African Images

Global Issues

General Editors: **Bruce Kapferer**, Professor of Anthropology, University College London and **John Gledhill**, Lecturer in Anthropology, University College London

This series addresses vital social, political and cultural issues confronting human populations throughout the world. The ultimate aim is to enhance understanding – and, it is hoped, thereby dismantle – hegemonic structures which perpetuate prejudice, violence, racism, religious persecution, sexual discrimination and domination, poverty, and many other social ills.

ISSN: 1354-3644

Previously published books in the series:

Michael Herzfeld
The Social Production of Indifference: Exploring the Symbolic Roots of Western Bureaucracy

Judith Kapferer
Being All Equal: Difference and Australian Cultural Practice

African Images

Racism and the End of Anthropology

Peter Rigby

BERG

Oxford · Washington, D.C.

First published in 1996 by
Berg
Editorial offices:
150 Cowley Road, Oxford, OX4 1JJ, UK
22883 Quicksilver Drive, Dulles, VA 20166, USA

Berg is an imprint of Oxford International Publishers Ltd.

Library of Congress Cataloging-in-Publication Data

A catalogue record for this book is available from the Library of
Congress.

British Library Cataloguing-in-Publication Data

A catalogue record for this book is available from the British Library.

Cover Photograph: © Milton Rogovin, Buffalo, New York.

ISBN 1 85973 196 1 (Cloth)
      1 85973 102 3 (Paper)

Typeset by JS Typesetting, Wellingborough, Northants.
Printed in the United Kingdom by WBC Book Manufacturers,
Bridgend, Mid Glamorgan.

Contents

Contents

Preface

In this book, I attempt a brief anthropological, or, if you like, ethnographic, study of a prominent group of Western (Euro-American) scientists and intellectuals. While it would be most desirable for such a project to be based upon first-hand fieldwork among these selected academics in the classical anthropological tradition (see "Theoretical Coda," below), my particular interests and somewhat radical approach to the social sciences, as well as the exigencies of an academic career, have precluded my obtaining the time, opportunity, or funding for such an exercise in empirical investigation.

However, with indignation as part of my motive, I fully concur with Laura Nader's trenchant comment, first published in 1969, upon scientific adequacy in anthropology (1974:289):

> If we look at the literature based upon field work in the United States, we find a relatively abundant literature on the poor, the ethnic groups, the disadvantaged; there is comparatively little field research on the middle class and very little first hand work on the upper classes. Anthropologists might indeed ask themselves whether the entirety of field work does not depend upon a certain power relationship in favor of the anthropologist, and whether indeed such dominant–subordinate relationships may not be affecting the kinds of theories they are weaving. What if, in reinventing anthropology, anthropologists were to study the colonizers rather than the colonized, the culture of power rather than the culture of the powerless, the culture of affluence rather than the culture of poverty.

And, I may add, the culture of the rulers, rather than that of the ruled.

Many anthropologists *have* been asking themselves these questions (e.g. Diamond 1974; Fabian 1983; Jackson 1989), but few have translated their discomfort into fieldwork "perspectives gained from studying up," preferring or being obliged to remain upon a theoretical level. While others have attempted to carry out such empirical studies (see Siwolop 1991; Burkhalter 1991 for some discussion), their necessary involvement with the aims, methods, and values of the economically powerful with whom they work mostly vitiates any really critical stance in the sense advocated by Nader. There are exceptions to this rule, such as the work of Traweek (1988); however, as Sandra Harding points out (1989:17), "there are occasional 'anthropologies' of the powerful in the West . . . but they are revolutionary; they must draw attention to the irony of their project in order to locate it in a comprehensible intellectual terrain for conventional Western audiences."

In lieu of any fieldwork on my own part, then, and in keeping with the legitimacy currently afforded the investigation of texts and textuality in anthropological discourse (Manganaro 1990; Clifford and Marcus 1986; Marcus and Fischer 1986; Clifford 1988; etc.), I deal here with the published works of the intellectuals and scientists targeted (how I love that word when it is aimed at the movers and shakers, rather than the moved and the shaken!) in this study. In order to understand what characterizes this particular set of academics and public figures, I selected a small number of texts. As Archie Mafeje perceptively notes in his epistemological "decoding" of a set of anthropological writings on the "inter-lacustrine states" of Africa (1991:iii). "A finite number of texts by the best exponents of each branch of knowledge sufficed. The same could be said of literary criticism. The essence is not the number of texts that one has read but how well one understands them."

Finally, since the purpose of this book is to examine the *broader* implications and consequences of intellectual work, not only in anthropology but in other fields related to the study of human beings (Part II), I feel I am fully justified in turning a critical anthropological (theoretical and political) gaze upon these writings. In answer to the question, "Can anthropology cope with these urgent issues?" I suggest that it may do so *only* if it abandons its commitment to a position of a positivist, empiricist, autonomous enquiring subject and adopts a critical and dialectical framework of knowledge (see "Theoretical Coda"). This may be achieved only by using the kinds of thinking and knowledge (that is, their dialectical forms) to which receptive anthropologists have been exposed in the predominantly non-capitalist societies in which they have lived or been brought up. I refer in this book mainly to African societies, for reasons given below. Non-social science readers may omit the "Coda" without missing the main argument!

Introduction

In a remarkably insightful book on cultural studies in Britain and America, Patrick Brantlinger notes (1990:147) that, "one obvious characteristic women share with both the working class and racial 'minorities' is that they are in actual fact a majority. Of course in certain communities and places around the world, men outnumber women, but the world population statistics tell another story. The same is true of the 'non-white' or non-European races of the world: the populations of Asia and Africa together account for over 70% of the world's total." So, too, the "working class," or those "who perform physical labor for wages or . . . produce food from land they do not legally own," are in the global majority.

Given the views of the scientists and intellectuals that follow in this book, they perhaps would be forgiven for not being too happy with these numbers. But these facts and figures raise interesting questions, and Brantlinger puts them succinctly (1990:147–8):

> But how does it come about that [the terms race, class, and gender] are perceived in the dominant culture [of the West] as relevant to "minorities" instead of majorities? How has the map of the world become so distorted in, for example, traditional humanities fields that questions of class, gender, and race seem marginal, "special" topics for seminars and graduate courses, perhaps, but not for the main agenda? These categories signify the *major* forms of division and difference between people. Understanding their historical, social construction, their complex interconnections, and their effects on "everyday life" and the formation of "subjectivities" is the chief aim of oppositional criticism.

Furthermore, in current discussions of multi-culturalism in the United States and Europe, the dominant white, male culture is never placed as "the Other," whose peculiar "differences" need to be explained to anyone. It is only "minorities" (Africans, African Americans, Black Englishmen, Asians, Native Americans) who constitute the Other (Azoulay 1994:23; Stinson-Fernandez 1994).

Anthropology, then, as the "science of man," must surely make these terms the center of its theoretical, methodological, and discursive practices as well as its politics; but in forms diametrically opposed to those exposed and criticized in this book. The study of gender issues is now established in most anthropology departments, although its increasing struggle has suffered recent setbacks in the crypto-fascist politics of the capitalist crisis in Europe, Britain, and the United States. Class analysis remains the work of a few dedicated but increasingly isolated anthropologists, and the study of "race," with some recent exceptions to be considered later, lies buried in the pseudo-scientific mythology being touted by sociobiology and related varieties of biological reductionist determinism as "science." It is an examination of the latter that forms Part I of this book.

Although racism, class exploitation, and gender discrimination are closely interconnected, they cannot be reduced to one another. Neither can racism be reduced to "ethnicity," a popular escape route for many American intellectuals, including "neo-conservative" African Americans such as Thomas Sowell (1983). As San Juan persuasively argues (1992:5):

> Race, not ethnicity, articulates with class and gender to generate the effects of power in all its multiple protean forms. Ethnicity theory elides power relationships, conjuring an illusory state of parity among bargaining agents. It serves chiefly to underwrite a functionalist mode of sanctioning a given social order. It tends to legitimize a pluralist but hierarchical status quo. Ellis Cashmore (1984) correctly points out that while ethnicity designates a collective sense of shared experiences underlying group solidarity, a sense of inclusiveness which grounds identity (*ethnos* etymologically denotes people or nation), race implies peoples and structures in historical processes of dissociation and exclusion that have distinguished the trajectory of Western civilization particularly since the European colonization of the Middle East, Africa, Asia, and the Americas.

I focus in this book on racism, with particular reference to Africa and peoples of African descent in the United States, the Caribbean, and Latin America. This is because, although white racism affects *all* "non-white" peoples, Africans and people of African descent are the particular targets of the resurgence of a neo-scientistic racism, as well as continuing forms of distorted anthropological and popular representation.

Anthropologists rightly pride themselves on their ability to analyze, understand, and explain mythological and symbolic systems, yet they seldom address those associated with the provenance of their own discipline and the political economy and culture of its own gestation and development. "Where anthropology's gaze is transfixed by the [diminished] Other, philosophy is obsessed with the *individual Euro-American self*, and with what it can know and make happen" (Sandra Harding 1989:17, my emphasis). This self-obsession precludes reflexive self-examination. One of the most widespread, systematic, and dangerous of these Western myths is the concept of "race" (Montagu: 1964, 1974), upon which the edifice of racism is constructed.

This has not always been the case. The founder of professional anthropology in the United States, Franz Boas, as his intellectual association with W.E.B. Du Bois attests, was profoundly concerned with countering the racist ideologies rampant in the anthropology of the time, as were some of his students. (This, of course, does not mean that Boas entirely escaped the effects of race discourses.) So, also, have some of the more unorthodox contemporary anthropologists, such as Stanley Diamond, Ashley Montagu, and Margaret Mead, as well as historians of anthropology such as George Stocking, been concerned with the issues of race and racism in anthropology (cf. also Lévi-Strauss 1961).

The primary reason why anthropologists have tended to avoid the topics of race and racism (but see Shanklin 1994), or have reduced them to "ethnic groups" and "ethnicity," is that they do not recognize that racism was historically one of the fundamental constituent elements of the rise of capitalism, bourgeois culture, *and alienated science*, and is *still necessary for their reproduction in their present form*. Racism, particularly expressed towards Africans, arises with the birth of capitalism and its attendant imperialism and colonialism. Although Lenin, in his remarkable pamphlet written in 1917, fully realized that "imperialism emerged as the development and direct continuation of the fundamental characteristics of capitalism in general" (1970:87), he was concerned with issues other than the early history of capitalism in the sixteenth century, or else his little book might better have been entitled

Imperialism: the First and Highest Stage of Capitalism!

In fact, as Jaffe pointedly explains, the very *ideas* of "European" and "European civilization" arose in conjunction with the exploitation of Africa and the growing need to justify it, by fabricating Africans as "non-human others" who *deserved* to be maltreated (Walvin 1973). As this issue is crucial to my later development of the distorted "Other" in bourgeois culture and science, I quote him at some length (Jaffe 1985:46):

> With capitalism arose Europe, and with Europe the myth of "European civilization" – a civilization based on African slavery, American plantations, Asian spices, precious metals from all three "non-European" continents – based, too, on Indian numerals, Arab algebra, astronomy, and navigation . . . and Chinese gunpowder, paper, and compasses. This non-European European civilization was the *narcissus-like admiration of its own conquests*. The sword, gunfire, murder, rape, robbery, and slavery formed the real material basis for the idea of European superiority (emphasis added).

But there was more than "African slavery" involved in this identity-formation of white, Western males; the very depreciation of the African/black Other is itself a denial of *reality* (the unity of all humankind), paralleled on the level of history and society as the almost universal denials by white Americans of the African content of their "Americanness" itself. I return to this point again.

While all peoples to some extent historically construct images of themselves in relation to different "Others," at both group and individual level, capitalist Europe had to *deny* the essential *equality* of this dialectical relation: but at the cost of denying simultaneously the universal validity of dialectical thinking itself (Sartre 1976). The myth of the superior European (white) male on the one hand, and the constitution of the solipsistic autonomous (individual) subject (the "narcissistic self-admiration") on the other, *demands* a diminished and humiliated "Other."

Jaffe continues (1985:46):

> It was out of this process that the very idea of a European man arose, as an idea that did not exist even in etymology before the 17th Century. Before the slave trade in Africa there was neither a Europe nor a European. Finally, with the European arose the myth of European superiority and separate existence as a special species or "race"; there arose indeed the myth of race in general, unknown to mankind before

– even the word did not exist before the lingua franca of the Crusades – the particular myth that there was a creature called a European which implied, from the beginning, a "white" man. *Colonialism, especially in Africa, created the concept and ideology of race.* Before capitalist-colonialism there were no races; but now, suddenly and increasingly, there were races: once born, the myth grew into a "reality."

Jaffe's exploration of the historical origins of the race concept is substantially supported by other major studies. There are no etymological precursors of "race" in classical Greek or Latin, and it appears in English in the late sixteenth century to describe breeds of animals; its first application to human beings dates to 1600 (Montagu 1964; Stepan 1982; Pandian 1985).

This mythical, historically constructed "reality," is now firmly a part of several projects in contemporary "scientific" investigations into intelligence, criminality, sexuality, and other cultural and "behavioral" phenomena, particularly in the United States. But, "since racism was at once the creature and the creator of Europe" and hence, as I have already mentioned, the "race" concept and racism are a "white" problem and not a "black" one (Fanon 1967; Césaire 1972), although their consequences are unfortunately most dire for peoples of African descent, we must study the white academics who purport to study race and not those they study.

What follows, then, is an anthropological investigation into the contemporary mythical science of race, as found among selected white (European) male scientists. I begin, therefore, with an examination of their ideas and activities concerning this mythological system (Part I); I then proceed to a theoretical consideration of how Africans may explain how otherwise rational human beings, who classify themselves as "white" and "Caucasoid" in their own work, continue to believe in such ideas, which are patently false to the anthropological observer. The "problem" of the rationality of belief has long been of major concern to anthropologists and philosophers, and appears here in especially potent form among a population which traces its thinking to the philosophy of the European Enlightenment (B. Wilson 1970; Jarvie and Agassi 1970; Lukes 1970; Evans-Pritchard 1937).

PART ONE

Of Niam-Niams, Troglodytes, and Unicorns

In 1851, a Frenchman called Francis de Castelnau published a book in which he claimed scientific evidence that there was a "tribe" in central Africa called "Niam-Niam" who had tails, and whose sole piece of furniture consisted of wooden benches with a hole in them to accommodate the tail (Cohen 1980:242; Miller 1985:3–4). This "evidence" was soon to be confirmed by another French gentleman, Louis Du Couret, who not only claimed to have traveled in the country of the Niam-Niams, but also provided an "eye-witness" picture of a Niam-Niam with his tail (Du Couret 1854). Du Couret was later exposed as a total charlatan; but this appellation should as well apply to Castelnau and his scientific colleagues in the Société de géographie de Paris, the Académie des sciences, and the Société orientale, for the *Oxford English Dictionary* (*OED*) tells us that a charlatan is "an empiric who claims to possess wonderful secrets" as well as "an assuming empty pretender to knowledge or skill; a pretentious impostor." The *Bulletin de la société de géographie* even published an article by de Castelnau entitled "Sur les Niam-Niam ou hommes queues," also in 1851.

Castelnau's evidence, prior to Du Couret's "eye-witness account," was based upon reports attributed to "Negroes of the Sudan." This attribution was convenient for the distinguished academicians of Paris for, when this evidence was shown to be completely false, it could be blamed upon the "Negroes of the Sudan." Indeed, many years later, social anthropologist E.E. Evans-Pritchard noted (1958:98) that the term Niam-Niam was sometimes used to describe the Azande people of southern Sudan and Zaire, and he comments, "The term 'Niam-Niam,' a foreign, perhaps Dinka, designation, is best avoided as it has been *used by Arabs and Europeans* without much discrimination to refer not only to both Azande and their subject-peoples but also to almost any people in the area under consideration. It was for some of them a very confused representation – cannibals, men with tails, etc." (my emphasis; cf. Bovin 1972:64–5).

This displacement (projection?) on to Africans of categorical terms propagated by Europeans (and Arabs) one hundred years before Evans-Pritchard's own gloss was repeated endlessly by European commentators on Africa; further examples are examined in Part II of this book. Here I must turn to definitions of the other mythical entities in the title of this section that have at times fired the European imagination.

A troglodyte, as every Westerner knows, is "one of various *races* or tribes of men . . . inhabiting caves or dens," as well as "anthropoid apes of the genus *Troglodytes*, as a gorilla or chimpanzee" (*OED*: my emphasis). Niam-Niams were, then, most likely troglodytes who, perhaps, hunted, or tried to domesticate, the unicorn. This animal, we learn from our trusty *OED*, is "a fabulous and legendary animal usually regarded as having the body of a horse with a single horn projecting from its forehead." One hopes, however, that the Niam-Niam-troglodytes never themselves suffered the indignity of being too closely associated with the unicorns they pursued: for the word also designated a cuckold.

CHAPTER ONE

The "Nightmare Republic" and the "Problem of the Underclass"

In an article, published in *Newsweek* on 17 June 1991, and entitled "Nature and the Male Sex," columnist George F. Will, nationally syndicated in the United States, waxed eloquent on a talk given by political scientist, James Q. Wilson. This lecture, on "Human Nature and Social Progress," was delivered at the American Enterprise Institute, and purported to "explain" the problems posed by contemporary urban youth. His piece, as well as the almost entire corpus of James Q. Wilson's other works, is representative of the barrage of racist prejudice and ideology, masquerading as "science" both physical (biological) and social (in this case, political), directed against "non-whites," particularly African Americans, by prominent whites in the United States and elsewhere in Western capitalist society.

The burden of the lecture by James Q. Wilson, at least according to Will, was that science had shown that "nature blundered badly in designing males," and hence that "socialization must contend against biology"; or, as Will prefaces his argument, "Uh oh. There is bad news on the nature-vs-nurture front." But this, of course, does not apply to *all* males, for, Wilson/Will avers, "the underclass problem arises from the incomplete and increasingly difficult task of socializing *some* males" (my emphasis). And we do not have to wait too long to see *who* these "some" are: young urban African Americans, although not identified in so many words. For it is here that Wilson's "social science" is brought into play.

We are told that the "ethic of character" embodied in nineteenth-century Victorian morality (a theme that James Wilson explores at length in a 1991 book: see below) was abandoned at a crucial moment in United States history. This moment was distinguished by two "epochal events: the great migration of Southern rural blacks to Northern cities and creation of a welfare state that made survival not dependent on work or charity . . . We have reproduced the historic conditions for a warrior class: separation of economic activity from family maintenance; children reared apart from fathers; wealth subject to predation; male status determined by combat and conquest."

The reader who begins to anticipate that the latter two features of contemporary historical conditions will lead Will (or Wilson) to a disquisition on the Savings and Loan scandal and the "Gulf War" is sadly mistaken. Instead, Will informs *Newsweek* readers that "The problems of the underclass, particularly male joblessness and illegitimate births, have been unresponsive to social policies." But not only that, because James Wilson says, "if mere incentives were the problem, low-income blacks would not be displaced from day labor by low-income Latinos; black-owned businesses would not be replaced by Korean-owned businesses in the same neighborhoods; low-income white women would become welfare recipients at the same rate as low-income black women; the average young black male would not be 10 times more likely to commit murder than a young white male." So what *is* "the problem"?

The apparently biological determination of sex differences ("natural science") in socialization, together with such ostensibly harmless social events as (black) population movements, conjoined in unholy intellectual matrimony to form the (unmentioned) scientific synthesis of sociobiology, not only "explains" for the Wills and Wilsons of the world the *creation* of an underclass in the United States, but also vitiates any recourse to socio-economic policies in solving its problems. *Why* this underclass has "not benefitted from our society's *generally successful strategies* for habituation of human beings through the do's and don'ts of daily life" (emphasis added) is apparently left open; but it is not really so. We do not have to go too far to uncover the insidious racism underlying James Wilson's argument, and Will knows it.

Although Will does not say it in so many words, and J.Q. Wilson is equally circumspect in his recent book (1991), their argument about crime, illegitimacy, and economic failure in the city is based upon an extensive literature and practice of a racist pseudo-science that maintains that African Americans are *genetically inferior* in every way to whites and Asians. Here, the "science" of *gender* differentiation in socialization is not so subtly transmuted into a blatant racist dogma; elsewhere in the work of Wilson and his associates and followers, the racism is more explicit, and I return to it in considerable detail. But the immediate question is: why are the other intellectuals, particularly anthropologists, silent?

In Will's article, Wilson is billed as president of the American Political Science Association at the time of his talk, to which distinction Mr. Will adds the accolade: "If James Q. Wilson is right, and memory runneth not to when he was not, the problem is that males are not naturally suited to civilization." But Will is too modest in his claims on behalf of Professor Wilson's reputation. Wilson's recent book (1991:209) puts the matter straight, for there we learn (if we did not know it already) that he has advised four U.S. presidents on crime, drug abuse, education, and other "crises in American culture." James Q. Wilson, "in addition to the 1981 Attorney General's Task Force on Violent Crime . . . served on the 1985–1990 President's Foreign Intelligence Advisory Board and the Commission on Presidential Scholars. He is Chairman of the Police Foundation." Wilson was Shattuck Professor of Government at Harvard University for twenty-six years and then went on to be James Collins Professor of Management and Public Policy at the University of California, Los Angeles; he is also chairman of the American Enterprise Institute's Council of Academic Advisers and a Member of its Board of Trustees.

So, it might be thought scandalous to accuse so distinguished an intellectual and public figure of racism. But this would be so only if the accusation were untrue; and it is not. It might also be asked why I have spent so much time and space on the undeserving case of James Q. Wilson. In fact, I intend to spend some more of both on him, for reasons that will become clear. We will see that we do not need the Ku Klux Klan or the "bad" skinheads to tell us about the illusion of a hierarchy of "races" and their supposedly different forms of social and cultural behavior, varied propensities towards criminality and sexuality, or inferiority–superiority in "intelligence." The job is being much more effectively done, certainly in terms of powerful influences upon the public psyche, by the respectable establishment of leading scientists, intellectuals, and public figures (see Montagu 1974) as illustrated in the *Newsweek* exposure already discussed.

Although a significant part of James Q. Wilson's academic career has been devoted to furthering the cause of biologically reductionist arguments for explaining the ills (particularly crime) of contemporary United States society, these arguments are carefully arrayed in an objective style, scientific language, and sophistry. Not so those of his colleagues, who espouse the same ideology and do the basic dirty work of "research," as we shall see. But first I must say some more on Wilson himself.

In the latest formulation of his argument, the first step is to assert that crime and criminality, while perhaps having economic links in the past, no longer have any relationship to socio-economic forces and politics in contemporary capitalist society. Here is this formulation (Wilson 1991:28):

> One can perhaps put the matter . . . strongly: whereas in the nineteenth century property crime was linked to the *business cycle*, today it is not. If true, that represents a profound change in the relationship between human behavior and historical forces. *Criminality has been decoupled from the economy* (emphasis added).

One may be excused for showing some surprise that Wilson equates "the economy" (or at least its most important aspects) with "the business cycle," even if it is bourgeois capitalist society he is talking about. But he wants to make it absolutely clear that he is not making a mistake. He states emphatically that, "Even the scholars who find evidence that economic factors have some effect on contemporary crime rates concede that the 'major movements in crime rates during the last half century cannot be attributed to the business cycle'," and to clinch this he refers to the work of Cook and Zarkin (1985) and, of course, *himself* and Cook (1978).

Next, we are told that the apotheosis of "civilization" is represented by the nineteenth century, presumably in Europe and the United States (although this is left unsaid), which, according to Norbert Elias ("the German sociologist"), "witnessed the full flowering of the civilizing process, that is, the acceptance of an ethos that attached great importance to the control of self-indulgent impulses." Today, alas, "matters could scarcely be more different" (Wilson 1991:28–9, 31). This collapse of "middle-class values" allegedly began in the 1920s and, with a short recess ("time out for a depression and a war"; neither, apparently, caused by this very lapse in moral values), resumed with a vengeance in the late 1960s (Wilson 1991:31–2).

We are to believe, according to James Wilson, that all through the nineteenth century and until the 1920s, (white) Euro-Americans of all classes demonstrated the "great importance [of] the control of self-indulgent impulses." Conveniently forgotten here, of course, is the fact that the nineteenth century and the early years of the twentieth were the period of the greatest Western imperialist expansion ever known, during which the colonized ("darker," "non-white") peoples of the world were subjected to the most horrifying and uncountable number of often capricious atrocities and uncontrolled violence by these paragons of the "control of self-indulgent impulses." A history of these atrocities would fill a library were it to be properly told, and I mention but a handful: the slaughter of Indians during the so-called "Indian Mutiny" of 1857; the massacres of Jamaicans of African descent in the "Jamaican Rebellion" of 1865; and the wanton slaying of the Amazulu people in southern Africa in 1879.

The case of Haiti is also instructive, both for the racist notions generated and strengthened during the nineteenth-century and for its continuing "uses" in late twentieth-century racist discourses and foreign policy decisions in the United States and other Western countries.

Haiti became the first "Black Republic" in the western hemisphere after a historic revolution against the French-ruled plantation slave colony of Saint-Domingue, a struggle sparked by the French revolution of 1789 itself. The French were decisively expelled in 1803, and the revolution consolidated in 1804 (James 1963 [1938]). This event in itself, combined with the fact that the Haitian African slaves had triumphed over the intervention of the mighty Napoleon Bonaparte's army *and* the imperialist interests of the British and the Spanish in the area, not only made Haiti the target of continual military interventions from Western capitalist countries (particularly the United States), but also became, for nineteenth-century white racists, a symbol of an African/Black "Other," whose freedom might inspire other insurrections and revolutions by peoples of African descent in the Caribbean and the United States itself. Haiti therefore had to be incessantly attacked and misrepresented. After tricking Toussaint L'Ouverture into being arrested, the French transported him to a prison in France where, owing to brutal ill treatment, he died on 7 April 1803. The French had attempted to break the incredible bravery and fortitude of the Haitian revolutionaries by demonizing

Toussaint; they failed, and the revolution, though irreparably damaged, was successful (James 1963 [1938]).

Throughout the nineteenth century and up to the present, the Western capitalist powers have tried to destroy the potential of the Haitian revolution as well as to vilify the people themselves. As James phrases it (1963 [1938]:362), "The balked greed of Bonaparte and the French bourgeoisie, their hatred of the 'revolted slave' who had ruined their plans, can be judged from the brutality with which they persecuted [Toussaint]."

But the real point at issue is that the racist attitudes displayed towards Haiti and Haitians by the white, Western, capitalist world from the beginning of the nineteenth century remain in force today, albeit in modified form. This "symbolic function" of Haiti as a despised Black Republic in the Western world, challenging the latter's global supremacy, took on greater and greater importance and continues to justify cruel and racist treatment of Haitians. In his excellent study of the Haitian predicament, Paul Farmer expresses these issues as follows (Farmer 1994:226):

> From the arrival of Columbus to the coup of 1991 [when Bertrand Aristide, the first democratically elected President Haiti had ever had, was overthrown after seven months in office], Haiti has had many uses. Some of these are obvious. Certainly, the plantations established by the French, the great extractive machines that transformed sweat and blood into sugar and gold, did little but turn chattel labor into exportable wealth . . . Independence changed much, but not all. The land itself, the poor who tilled it, continued to yield the same bounty, and if the profits were not as great, they were hardly shared in a more equitable manner within Haiti. As seen from the outside, however, Haiti had become a completely different sort of symbol after 1804. In a monolithically racist world, Haiti was "the nightmare republic." Throughout the nineteenth century, European and American visitors to Haiti culled material for best-selling texts that told readers what they most wanted to hear. The hypothesis to be confirmed, invariably, was that blacks were incapable of self-rule. Haitians had been quick to understand that the country would be punished for daring to suggest otherwise: "To fully appreciate the origin of the unceasing calumnies of which Haiti has been made the target," observed one Haitian diplomat in 1907, "one must go back to the very first days of her existence and call to mind the circumstances under which she started life as an independent country."

This diplomatic and cultural ostracism of Haiti, however, did not assuage the thirst for profits in the Western capitalist world. As Michel-Rolph Trouillot aptly puts it (1990:50):

> The birth of an independent state on the ashes of a Caribbean colony was seen as a major threat by racist rulers in Western Europe and in the United States. Given the climate of the times and the general acceptance of Afro-American slavery in the white world, the Haitian revolution was equal to such modern day events as the Vietnamese victory, the "loss" of "French" Algeria, or the rise of socialist Cuba a few miles off the coast of Florida. Accordingly, the United States and most European governments imposed a diplomatic and political blockade on the new state. But profit and *raison d'état* were nevertheless reconcilable, and some merchants from Britain, France, Germany, and New England continued to trade with Haiti whenever it was in their best interests. Indeed, the international context favored the foreign traders by reducing the bargaining power of the Haitian middlemen, who were allowed no official representation in the countries they traded with (*Le Télégraphe* 1819).

The "glorious nineteenth century," then, was hardly conducive to Haiti's positive transformation into a modern democracy, and Farmer elegantly notes (1994:228), "Haiti took on greater and greater symbolic functions. As the fruits of independence rotted on the vine, Haiti became a cautionary tale of great relevance to all colonial powers with holdings in the New World." British envoy Sir Spencer St. John set the tone in his memoir of *Hayti or the Black Republic* [published in 1884]:

> I know what the black man is, and I have no hesitation in declaring that he is incapable of the art of government, and that to entrust him with framing and working the laws for our islands is to condemn them to inevitable ruin. What the negro may become after centuries of civilized education I cannot tell, but what I know is that he is not fit to govern now.

The United States intervened militarily in Haitian affairs throughout the nineteenth century, and continues to do so in the twentieth. They sent U.S. warships into Haitian waters in 1849, 1851, 1857, 1858, 1865, 1866, 1867, 1868, 1869, 1876, 1888, 1891, 1892, 1902, 1903, 1904, 1905, 1906, 1907, 1908, 1909, 1911, 1912, and 1913, culminating in a full-scale imperialist Marine occupation of the state from 1915 to 1934 (Farmer 1994:89). During the latter period, the U.S. Marines brutally destroyed a popular peasant liberation movement called the Cacos, and, in a maneuver reminiscent of the luring of Toussaint to his death in 1802–3, the leader of the Cacos movement, Charlemagne Péralt, was assassinated by the Marines in 1919, and his mutilated body put on public display in Port au Prince. The United States Marines, on the admission of their own officers, "hunted the Cacos like pigs," and a Major Smedley Butler who organized the slaughter so impressed the U.S. government he was awarded the Congressional Medal of Honor (Farmer 1994:311). It seems that one need not go too far to find the precedents for the contemporary killing fields of Haiti at the close of the twentieth century!

During the marine occupation of Haiti, that would-be pillar of the intellectual establishment in Washington, the *National Geographic*, happily joined in the racist attack upon the Haitian people and their culture, its staff writers referring in a 1920 article to Haitian peasants as "unthinking black animals of the interior." They continued (Farmer 1994:228–9):

> In this carnival of barbarism religion also had its place. Cannibalism and the black rites of voodoo magic of the African jungles were revived in all their horror, and the sacrifices of children and of animals to the mumbo jumbos of the local wizard was practiced in the appropriate seasons. Poisoning and praying to death became the mode, and missionaries to the island report that fully four-fifths of all the population are either active believers in or hold in fear the spell of witch doctors.

Farmer goes on to point out that it is nothing new that "associations between Haitians and infectious diseases are particularly strong" in the United States, noting that in the same edition of the *National Geographic* (1920), the claim was made that "it is estimated that 87% of the entire population were infected by contagious diseases." Just as AIDS was said at one time to have originated in Haiti, a distinction later ascribed to Africa (see Part II below), so too did Europeans in the sixteenth century insist that syphilis originated in Haiti (Farmer 1994:229).

The point to be reiterated is that, just as with capitalist slavery in the United States and the Caribbean, the colonial and neo-colonial exploitation of Africa and the constant Western "counterinsurgency" interventions in the contemporary "Third World" generate racist dogma.

Elsewhere in the world during the nineteenth century, we may add the genocidal policies of the "civilized" German colonizers in various parts of Africa: for example, the policy of extermination against the Ovaherero in Southwest Africa (Namibia) from 1894 to 1918 and against the peoples of German East Africa (Tanzania) during the "Maji-maji Rebellion." Then there was the rape of the Congo and the massacre and mutilation of its peoples by King Leopold II of Belgium, between 1887 and 1908, all in the interests of capitalist profit, in which such giants of American capitalism as J.P. Morgan, John D. Rockefeller, Thomas F. Ryan, and Daniel Guggenheim did not hesitate to share.

What, then, was the *content* of this nineteenth-century white civilization as expressed in its *culture*? Patrick Brantlinger, a leading researcher into the Victorian and Edwardian periods, notes succinctly that "Imperialism, understood as an evolving but pervasive set of attitudes and ideas towards the rest of the world, influenced all aspects of Victorian and Edwardian culture." He deals with the period 1830 to 1914, including the "New Imperialism" of the later nineteenth century, which "manifested itself in the Scramble for Africa and other parts of the world that still remained to be overrun by the European bearers of light and the Maxim gun" (Brantlinger 1988:8,14). Peter Gay has recently made the telling point (Gay 1993:69) that "the most interesting reasons the nineteenth century advanced for feeding collective narcissism [and elaborating hatred towards the collective "Other"] were modern. It injected what it touted as scientific rationales for hating and despising outsiders. What came to dominate these rationales for aggression was the argument from race."

For James Wilson, however, these colonial barbarities do not constitute "crimes" in his sense of the term; perhaps he may even see them as part of the "civilizing process" of the nineteenth century, as it was so successfully touted by the imperialist powers of the time and their intellectual and missionary apologists. But, as we shall see, there is more to Wilson's self-proclaimed identification with nineteenth-century values than this.

Compound these atrocities with the Atlantic slave trade and capitalist slavery in the Americas, upon which Western capitalism (particularly in the United States) was built from the sixteenth century until well into the nineteenth, and the number of Africans

and people of African descent who were sacrificed upon the altar
of the Western "ethos of self-control" (Wilson 1991:28) runs into
untold millions. The three centuries of the trans-Atlantic trade
alone amount to the unconstrained exploitation of, at the very
least, 15 million Africans, and the murder of an unknown number
(but probably twice that or more) by the conditions in the "Middle
Passage."

In fact, in the nineteenth century, the abominations of the trade
were even worse than before. As Davidson points out (1992:22),
"in the middle years of the nineteenth century, the mortality [of
the Middle Passage] was even higher still, for the old 'close packing'
of the legal trade, horrible enough as that had been, had given
way to the dense packing of the smuggling trade." Some slave ships
during this period, with slave-deck clearances of fourteen inches,
were intended for children only. One such ship, apprehended by
HMS *Fantome* in 1842, contained 105 slaves, all of whom, except
for a girl of fourteen, were under nine and over four years of age
(Forbes 1969 [1849]), quoted in Davidson 1992:22–3).

Unlike the demise of Wilson's "civilizing process" of the
nineteenth century and the weakening of "moral habituation" in
the twentieth, however, the racism invented by white men to
rationalize and justify the vicious exploitation of black men,
women, and children has not died or even faded away; it has simply
taken different forms. Thus the myths upon which it is based still
have their power, although it is manifested in a functionally
different manner. This racism is as ideologically necessary to the
reproduction of the contemporary United States social formation
as it was during the period of slavery, and therefore has constantly
to be re-invented (Fields 1990). In this process, establishment
intellectuals such as Wilson and his acolytes play a pivotal role. So
let me return once again to his "argument."

We have seen that Wilson asserts that the period after the 1920s
is marked by the "decoupling" of crime from the economy
("business cycles"), a decline in the power of the "civilizing process"
through "changed attitudes," and a weakening in the ethos of
"moral habituation." Up to this point, the argument is ostensibly
sociological and general; I shall show later that this is not so. In
this particular book (Wilson 1991:101–3), the race concept is used
explicitly to designate a "black problem" as more and more African
American students enter the high school he himself attended when
there were no blacks there. This ostensibly innocuous use of race

categories is racist enough, designating a "black problem" where in reality there is a "white one." But this need not detain us here. The more masked use of "race" as a causal explanatory element elsewhere in the book is much more important.

Expanding upon his postulate of the attrition of moral habituation, Wilson again effects a perhaps not so subtle transmutation in purpose. I must quote him *in extenso*, both to show that I am not distorting his case, and also to prepare the reader for my subsequent critique. This is what he says (1991:35):

> [The] reduction in routinized moral habituation probably affects everyone to some degree, but for *most people* the effect is minor because their parents and peers have *intuitively rewarded decency and punished selfishness* and because people have *entered markets and neighborhoods* that reinforced the lessons of their early training. But some lack the earlier training or the later environment, and so become vulnerable to the self-indulgent tone of modern culture (my emphasis).

So far, the argument again seems to emphasize sociological factors which, however weak the sociology, could obviously be linked to the political economy of class in the United States, even if the economy is now reduced to "markets." But having already "decoupled" crime, as well as its other sociological correlates, from "historical forces," as we have seen, Wilson now shows his real intentions, and we are next told that (1991:35–6):

> Black Americans have been especially vulnerable in this regard [that is, to "the self-indulgent tone of modern culture"]. Roger Lane has described how black homicide rates in Philadelphia rose from the mid- to the late-nineteenth century, roughly doubling at a time when . . . the overall homicide rate was falling. *Other immigrant groups*, notably the Irish and the Italians, had high murder rates when first settling in that city, but soon their rates began to fall. Lane attributes the black increase to their systematic exclusion from the economic life of the city, an exclusion that placed the black middle class in a hopeless position: its commitment to respectability was threatened by whites (who refused to reward respectability with legitimate economic advancement) and *by other blacks (who scorned respectability by creating profitable and status-conferring criminal enterprises)* (emphasis added).

James Q. Wilson might, of course, concede that African Americans were hardly an "immigrant group among others," and that some Italian- and Irish-Americans (as with other "ethnic groups") have excelled, even up to the present, in "creating profitable criminal enterprises," so that perhaps this phenomenon tells us more about U.S. society as a whole than about the African American community. But these issues are not really his concern, which is to single out blacks and their imputed "propensity for crime." If, for Wilson, history and political economy, prejudice against and exploitation of blacks in the United States, do *not* explain higher crime rates in the black community, then what does?

James Wilson's aim here is clearly to separate African Americans from *all other groups or categories of persons*, including the Irish, Italians, "Asians," and other "ethnicities," particularly in relation to crime, and to impute a genetic basis for the difference. In the book under scrutiny, the argumentative focus is on "culture," but (as I will show) the *reasons* for culturally differentiating blacks from all other Americans are derived from his other works (especially Wilson and Herrnstein 1985) and from those of his followers, who constantly refer to him in their quest for respectability.

Wilson's argument (and that of others) is that African Americans are *culturally* deprived because they are *genetically* inferior, a state of affairs caused by the fact that they are not as *advanced as whites in evolutionary terms*; whites, in turn, are not as advanced as Asians. But more of this later. Here I must pursue the Wilson of 1991 a little further (1991:36):

> The folk culture of urban blacks, as many observers have noted, was and is aggressive, individualistic, and admiring of semiritualistic insults, sly tricksters, and masculine display. This popular culture may have been a reaction against the repressive and emasculating aspects of slavery; *whatever its origins*, it was not a culture productive of *moral capital* off which people could live when facing either *adversity or affluence* (emphasis added).

This insulting characterization of African American culture allows Wilson to ignore the fact that aggression and individualism are immanent in capitalism and that "masculine display" is not peculiar to African Americans (see below). But it also states explicitly that African American culture cannot handle adversity *or* affluence. The *only* answer left open by Wilson's line of thought has been there all along: the postulated genetic gulf between Africans and people of African descent on the one hand, and whites and Asians on the other. The latter two "races," while somewhat different, are genetically much "closer" to each other than either is to Africans. James Wilson continues:

The contrast between black popular culture and that of other repressed minorities – Asian-Americans and Hispanic-Americans – has often been remarked. This may help explain why, as Lane notes, black crime rates are higher than Hispanic ones, even in cities where black income is significantly higher than Hispanic income. Glenn Loury has complained of the continuing failure of middle-class blacks to provide visible moral leadership on such issues as crime, teenage pregnancy, and single-parent families. While one can appreciate the desire of black leaders *to avoid giving ammunition to racists* by publicly discussing the moral decay of some parts of the black community, in the long run silence will be self-destructive (emphasis added).

Wilson, clearly, does not need any further ammunition for *his* racism; he is quite content with what he has from his own researches and those of numerous others. Elsewhere in his work and that of his colleagues, Wilson is not at all reticent about being explicit on what he claims are the causes of imputed black cultural deprivation, moral decay, crime, etc. But even here he cannot resist adding insult to injury by invoking the name of W.E.B. Du Bois (misspelled "DuBois" to boot) in "support" of his invidious assertions (1991:35). The argument of "cultural deprivation" is also central to Hallpike's racist anthropology (1979: see below).

In order to explore the extent to which this mythology of scientific racism afflicts the bourgeois academic community in the West, we must now turn to the ramifications of Wilson's work and the uses to which it has been put by others in other disciplines, as illustrated, for example, in his collaboration with Richard Herrnstein (Wilson and Herrnstein 1985). The latter is a dedicated proponent of the racist strategies of the educational psychologist Arthur Jensen and the physicist William Shockley in the United States, and of H.J. Eysenck and his colleagues in England. It should be noted first, however, that the writings of the latter intellectuals themselves are not a thing of the past, confined to the late 1960s when Jensen published his first article on the issue of race and IQ (1969). For example, a publisher no less reputable than The Free Press (Macmillan) brought out Jensen's *Straight Talk About Mental Tests* in 1981, in which he recapitulates his assertions that blacks are genetically inferior in intelligence as indicated by IQ tests.

I will not spend any time on *this* particular branch of Western intellectual sorcery and magic (see Flynn's over-polite 1980 critique) except to note that Jensen strenuously defends himself against the charge of racism by recourse to the usual stratagem of assuming the mask of "science." He states (1981:207), "The scientific study of mental or behavioral differences between races, openly recognizing the possibility that genetic factors may play a role, cannot be called racist. It would be just as illogical to condemn the recognition of physical differences between races as racist." In Jensen's terms, this "scientific study" *is* racist – just as much as was polygenist (and virtually psychotic) Louis Agassiz's statement on human races in 1850 (Gould 1981:44–5). This is because the *categories* upon which it is based ("race," "physical differences between races," "intelligence") are the spurious inventions of capitalism and colonialism.

But "thereby hangs a tale" (if not a "tail"): for the fact is that the "physical differences" between the typological "races" used by James Wilson, Jensen, and the numerous others to follow, are *historically and conventionally constructed* mythic categories, which have virtually nothing to do with the distribution of significant genetic polymorphisms among human populations. The idea that the conventional tripartite division of humanity into "Negroid," "Caucasoid," and "Mongoloid" is based upon the scientific evidence of genetics is an absurd, continually reinvented and reiterated piece of racist propaganda itself, just as is the notion that IQ tests tell us anything significant about human beings (Montagu 1974; Lewontin 1982; Gould 1981; Stepan 1982; Rose, Kamin, and Lewontin 1984). Correlating the mythical categories of "race" and "IQ" is thus an exercise in mythological manipulation, and irrelevant to science. We may as well, as the title of this part of the present work suggests, spend the enormous sums of research money devoted to race and IQ studies upon an analysis of the behavioral characteristics of Niam-Niam-Troglodytes in their efforts to harness the energies of unicorns.

But the apparent need of Western whites constantly to reinvent the concept of "race" (and thus justify its concomitant racism) has left even Arthur Jensen behind. In closing his book, already mentioned, Jensen claims (1981:258) that:

> Racism is one of the major hindrances to the scientific study of racial variation in intelligence and other behavioral traits. Racism is the belief that human races can be distinctly ordered in a simple hierarchy in

terms of some global evaluation of inferior-superior . . . solely according to their racial origins or their socially defined racial group membership. There is nothing that would lend support to these racist beliefs.

But it is *precisely* such invidious evaluations and orderings of races that are the direct legacy of Jensen's and his colleagues' work, and that are now flourishing in the writings of James Q. Wilson, Herrnstein, Rushton, Ellis, and others. And it is to these that I now turn.

CHAPTER TWO

The Invention of the Three Human Races

I begin with what may be called a "state of the art" article produced by one of this group of researchers, particularly because it deals with genetics and crime, the area in which James Q. Wilson's writings have had a major impact (Wilson and Herrnstein 1985). In an imposing volume entitled *Crime in Biological, Social, and Moral Contexts*, edited by Ellis and Hoffman and published by Praeger in 1991, Glayde Whitney expounds on the "Possible Genetic Bases of Race Differences in Criminality."

In various other pieces to be considered below, it is not only criminality that is linked to racial differences; what is consistent in all of them, as we shall see, is that the "races" are ranked (from "superior" to "inferior") as in Orientals–whites–blacks; but blacks are relegated to the most "distant" position at the bottom, with Orientals/whites at the top, different but "close." But even more importantly, when IQ "rankings" are added to all these other "behavioral measures," an *evolutionary hypothesis* is, in earlier efforts (for example, Rushton and Bogaert 1987), advanced to explain them. This "hypothesis" is then "confirmed" in all subsequent articles, from about a year later, as a valid theoretical basis for "scientific" investigation, and used as such. Significantly, *all* of these articles refer for intellectual and political support to Wilson and Herrnstein's 1985 book.

I must note here that in what follows, I do not deal in depth with all the technical issues involved in these racially biased and outrageous researches; this is a task that has been adequately covered by numerous academics in the same fields as these authors (e.g. Lynn 1989a, 1989b; Flynn 1989; Cain and Vanderwolf 1990; Zuckerman 1990; Zuckerman and Brody 1988; and numerous others). It is my task, as I have already stated, to expose the mythical foundations of these exercises and the tenacity of their authors' beliefs in their claims to "science." Some technical discussion, however, is necessary.

The first methodological point that Whitney and these scientists of race must, of course, establish is that the three typological "races" are distinguished on genetically valid grounds. They freely admit themselves that the three categories they use have already been so designated for more than a hundred years, *long before the "advances"* of "the last few decades in biological research, increased knowledge of molecular biology, molecular genetics, and neuroscience" (Whitney 1990:144).

Here for the first time in their discourse (but not the last), scientific method is stood upon its head; and, as we shall see, this inversion invalidates everything that is built upon it. For the "three races" (however they are designated) were not initially distinguished on genetic grounds: there were no genetic grounds on which they could be determined at the time. In all these subsequent intellectual enterprises, genetic "differences" are adduced *ex post facto* to confirm an *a priori* typological classification. As the co-editor of the volume in which Whitney's article appears lamely suggests (Ellis 1990:41), "Three major racial groups have been recognized in both scientific and popular schemes – black, white, Oriental," this "recognition" being attributed to physical anthropologists and sociobiologists (Ogburn, Nimkoff, Garrison, Wallace, and Knowels). Glayde Whitney is more emphatic, identifying the three races (in his case, "Mongoloid, "Negroid," and "Caucasoid") as *subspecies*, which is, of course, totally erroneous (1990:134):

> *Race* is used in this chapter to refer to recognizable subpopulations of humans. The subdivision of a species into races is usually the result of relative geographical separation and consequent differential evolution among populations during the evolutionary history of the species. Given that we are considering *biological subspecies (races)*, a number of separate considerations are involved in addressing the possibility that there may be some genetic involvement in the causation of race differences in criminality (emphasis added).

All the texts discussed here use the same tripartite classification, differing only in terminology. Whitney and others give as their major reference in validation of their classifications the work of John R. Baker, whose book *Race* (1974) is considered by them the *locus classicus* on the matter, and whose status as a zoologist at Oxford University lends some transatlantic ivy-covered weight to more local efforts. I spend no more time on Baker's *puissance* to define the "three races" than to agree with Nancy Stepan that his book is a "vast, old-fashioned, and decidedly typological book," and to note further with her that Baker had an earlier career in "anti-communism, eugenics, and racist polemics" (Stepan 1982:189, 222. n.42). Most importantly, Baker's classifications are not even claimed to be (and certainly are not) modern, "gene-based" ones, whatever these may be.

But *how* "old-fashioned" this classification of human races really is still needs to be established. For our present purposes, we need go no further back than James Q. Wilson's nineteenth century with its "full-flowering of the civilizing process" and its "self-styled ethnologist of mid-nineteenth century France," Count Joseph Arthur de Gobineau (Miller 1985:16). Jean-Paul Sartre accurately identified Gobineau as "the father of racism" in its pseudo-scientific and modern forms; his patriarchal ghost, if not his genetic inheritance, still haunts the corridors of particular establishment academies. For it is enlightening to note that, in 1853–5, Gobineau, long before any scientific genetics was dreamed of, divided humanity into "three great races . . . black, yellow, and the white," the "greatness" here denoting quantity rather than quality, especially where the "black race" was concerned.

But not only this: for Gobineau also presaged the contemporary "discovery" by our modern race scientists that the greatest "distance" between these races was between "black" and "yellow," with the former, of course, at the bottom and the latter at the top, and with alleged *sexual* differences being given a major role, an item faithfully exhumed by our contemporary scientific colleagues (Gobineau 1967:205–6; quoted in Miller 1985:17):

> The Melanin variety [Africans/blacks] is the humblest and lives at the bottom of the scale. The animalistic character etched in his loins imposes his destiny from the minute of conception. His fate holds him within the most limited intellectual scope. However, he is not a pure and simple brute, this Negro with a narrow and sloped forehead, who bears in the middle section of his brain the signs of grossly powerful energies. If these thinking facilities are poor or even null, he is

possessed, by his desire and also by his will, of an often terrible intensity
. . . The yellow race presents itself as an antithesis of this type. The
skull, instead of sloping backward, is inclined precisely forward . . . As
for character, none of the strange excesses so common among the
Melanins.

One hundred and forty years after Gobineau, Glayde Whitney
(1990:137) attempts to confirm the convergence between genetics
(a modern science) and racial diversity (an old typology) by
referring to a certain B.O.H. Latter (1980), who claims to
demonstrate that in genetic diversity "the largest difference was
that between the African and East Asian groups. The Caucasoid
versus African difference was 81 percent as large as the African–
East Asian, while the Caucasoid–East Asian value was 43 percent
of the African–East Asian difference." To drive home the "genetic
distance" factor between Africans and all other races (that is, the
rest of humanity, with the possible exception of the "Melanesians"
of the Western Pacific), Whitney also recruits studies by Stringer
and Andrews (1988), who "emphasize an African versus non-
African patterning of genetic differences" [and] summarize genetic
distances as indicating "a rather close Caucasoid–Mongoloid
relationship. The largest genetic difference was again between
Negroid–Mongoloid, with an intermediate Negroid–Caucasoid
genetic distance." The criteria used in this "rank ordering" of races
(they indiscriminately substitute the term "populations" for their
groupings of Mongoloids, Caucasoids, and Negroids) comprise a
list of "racial traits" grouped into five categories: intelligence;
maturation rate; personality and temperament; sexuality; and
social organization. The actual "traits" range from cranial capacity,
age of first intercourse, impulsivity, through size of genitalia, to
something called "law abidingness" (Rushton 1988:1010). This last
concept is attributed to Wilson and Herrnstein (1985).

At this point, one may legitimately ask: whatever happened to
everything between Gobineau and Whitney, as far as Whitney is
concerned, especially in response to the development of a science
of genetics? The answer to this important rhetorical question is,
of course, *nothing*: other than the application of increasingly
"sophisticated" ways of "proving scientifically" already entrenched
and distorted ideological categories. As all anthropologists know,
however, myths that still have crucial political, economic, social,
and psychological functions in ensuring the reproduction of the

societies in which they are espoused, and in which they act as "mythical charters," are not easily dislodged.

At any rate, as far as Whitney is concerned, all the evidence produced indicates that blacks (Africans, African Americans) are genetically more inclined to criminality than whites who, in turn, are more so predisposed than are Orientals (Whitney 1990:141), and this is the unstated conclusion of James Q. Wilson in his 1991 book to which I have already referred. "In summary," says Whitney, "many crime rate data are consistent in indicating substantial differences among major races with a rank ordering of blacks–whites–Orientals, as predicted from the separate literature addressing genetic differentiation among races."

Such a conclusion, that of a global rank ordering of the "races" in terms of inferiority–superiority, would fit neatly into Jensen's definition of racism (1981:258); but I have yet to come across any censure of Whitney on these grounds by Jensen or any of his colleagues and, I may venture to suggest, we are unlikely to see it. Here, of course, we can take some solace in the fact that the usual hierarchy of races is reversed, blacks being best at crime, followed by whites and Orientals in that order! This consolation, however, is short-lived; our genetic determinist warriors elsewhere associate criminality with low IQs, thereby confirming to their satisfaction the inverse hierarchy in this case.

CHAPTER THREE

Sexual Inhibition and the "Ethnographic Record"

But all this applies not only for crime and IQ: according to Rushton, Bogaert, and others, blacks are more different from whites and Orientals in all sorts of other genetically determined ways. The "rank ordering" of all the "desirable (civilized) characteristics," of course, place the races in the hierarchy Orientals–whites–blacks. Rushton and Bogaert (1987) begin with asserting racial differences in "sexual restraint" and "inhibited sexuality." That "restraint" and "inhibition" are *good* is established in the first paragraph of their article with a nod in the direction of Freud who, we are told, "noted a positive correlation between inhibited sexuality and the production of culture" (Rushton and Bogaert 1987:529). This emasculation of Freud's assertion (certainly it was not a "note"), as well as the fact that it initially applied to *individual differences*, are brushed under the carpet by spuriously arguing from individual to group without any theoretical justification. It should be noted in passing that this is in keeping with all bourgeois social theory based upon methodological individualism.

To cut a long story short, what this study purports to demonstrate is that this same rank ordering of races in all desirable (advanced) forms of sexual behavior is, as we have seen, upheld and related to other measurable "racial" traits, including cranial capacity, gamete production and dizygotic twinning, age of first pregnancy, aggressiveness (shades of James Q.Wilson on "black urban culture"), frequencies of sexual intercourse, permissive sexual attitudes, marital stability, mental health, and "law abidingness." In a later article, Rushton (1989:10) even treats us to a genetic racial theory of the origin of classes and the state! But more of that later.

From an anthropological point of view, it is interesting to note here that in their review of the literature in the process of substantiating their peculiar views, Rushton and Bogaert invoke what they call "the ethnographic record." This consists of references to a single, presumably authoritative, figure called "A French Army Surgeon," writing, for the record, in 1898 (but reprinted in 1972). He is described by Rushton and Bogaert (1987:536) as "a 30-year specialist in genitourinary diseases." In a position paper summarizing the "data," Rushton repeats verbatim his earlier piece with Bogaert and enthusiastically re-quotes this distinguished if anonymous figure from the glorious nineteenth century, on "African descended people" in contrast to Caucasians/ Orientals, as follows (Rushton 1988:1015):

> The ethnographic record (e.g. A French Army Surgeon, 1898/1972) makes reference to anatomical distinctions, including the placement of female genitals (Orientals highest, blacks lowest); angle and texture of erection (Orientals parallel to body, and stiff, blacks at right angles to body and flexible); size of genitalia (orientals smallest, blacks largest); salient muscularity, buttocks and breasts (Orientals least, blacks most).

And for "confirmation" of these "findings," who but Rushton and Bogaert (1987) are cited as one of two references? But, we may ask after all this breathlessly delivered quantitative information on body parts and functions, how *do* these genetic race-theory warriors *explain* to themselves the reasons for their racist agenda? And the final synthesis is provided, not unexpectedly, by the sociobiologists through what is called "differential r/K theory."

"r/K Selection," Lombroso, and the Capitalist "Science" of Racism

The theory of r/K selection was initially proposed in 1962 by, among others, the founding father of sociobiology, E.O. Wilson (MacArthur and Wilson 1967) to explain differences between species in evolutionary biology. It is best asserted in the words of one of its proponents, under the rubric of a "biosocial perspective" (Ellis 1990:43–4):

> The concept of *r/K selection* [is] an extension of modern (or gene-based) evolutionary theory. The concept refers to a continuum along which all living things (or, more precisely, the genes they carry) may be arrayed. In most general terms, r-selected organisms tend to produce large numbers of offspring that receive little or no parental care and are born after what tends to be a short gestation period. At the other end of the continuum, K-selected organisms normally produce few offspring in a lifetime and devote great time and energy to parental care (a basic form of altruistic behavior), thereby maximizing each offspring's reproductive potential.

On this continuum, organisms which produce a large number of offspring, have shorter gestation periods, larger numbers of miscarriages and higher neo-natal death rates, mature early sexually, have high fertility potential, copulate more frequently, have unstable sexual bondings, and have low parental investment and life expectancy are all "r-selected," and are *therefore lower on the evolutionary scale.*

Rushton, Bogaert, and their cohorts, however, apply r/K selection *within* the species *Homo sapiens* to "prove" that Africans and peoples of African descent are more "r-selected," while whites and Orientals are "K-selected" with the last "most K." Rushton then offers an "ecological" explanation for this evolutionary divergence of "races" (1985, 1989:8-12), an argument that would make any self-respecting ecological anthropologist blush with shame. The real burden of Rushton's project is, again, to "demonstrate" a "divergence time of about 110,000 years for the Negroid–non-Negroid split and about 41,000 years for the Caucasoid–Mongoloid split" (Rushton 1989:11).

These tired arguments need not detain us here. The entire Grand Guignol is demolished by Lynn (1989a, 1989b; and many others). In fact, in assessing Rushton's contention that IQ tests demonstrate the genetic inferiority of blacks, Lynn (1989b:32) uses Rushton's own data and argument to conclude that "blacks matched with high IQ whites are probably genetically superior because they had to overcome their environmental disadvantages" and the evidence supports "the genetic *equality* of blacks and whites" (original emphasis). Lynn concludes (1989b:32) that these researches on race contain "selective and biased descriptions of relevant literatures, and [misrepresent] some of the theory and data used" in their rebuttal.

But returning from early evolutionary speculations to contemporary problems such as crime, the r/K selection "theory" is used by others to "demonstrate" why blacks are supposedly more inclined to criminality than whites/ Orientals. Thus Ellis concludes (1990:44), "To account for criminality within this evolutionary scheme, *one need only assume* that (a) humans vary along the r/K continuum (even though, relative to the entire spectrum of life forms, the human species would be confined towards the K-end of the continuum) and (b) criminal behavior (at least in its victimful forms) is, to a substantial degree, a manifestation of r-selection" (my emphasis). The circularity of this proposition is immediately evident.

Unfortunately for Ellis and similarly-minded scientists, the "theory" that blacks are more criminally inclined than whites and Orientals because they are "lower" on the evolutionary scale is not merely the product of their twentieth-century scientistic sophistry. It is directly descended from the biological speculations of the nineteenth century, most specifically from Cesare Lombroso's ludicrous theories of criminality (1887). Stephen Gould's summary of Lombroso's theory, with the substitution of the word "genetic" for "anthropometric" data, could readily describe James Q. Wilson and Herrnstein's assertions about race and crime, as well as those of Ellis, Whitney, and numerous others (Gould 1981:124):

> Lombroso's theory was not just a vague proclamation that crime is hereditary – such claims were common in his time – but a specific *evolutionary* theory based upon anthropometric data. Criminals are evolutionary throwbacks in our midst. Germs of an ancestral past lie dormant in our heredity. In some unfortunate individuals, the past comes to life again. These people are innately driven to act as a normal ape or savage would, but such behavior is deemed criminal in our civilized society. Fortunately, we may identify born criminals because they bear anatomical signs of their apishness. Their atavism is both physical and mental, but the physical signs, or stigmata as Lombroso calls them, are decisive. . . . Anatomy, indeed, is destiny, and born criminals cannot escape their taint: "We are governed by silent laws which can never cease to operate and which rule society with more authority than the laws inscribed on our statute books. *Crime appears to be a natural phenomenon*" (Lombroso 1887:667; emphasis added).

Perhaps Lombroso was the first sociobiologist? With the difference that anatomical stigmata are now genetic traits, Lombroso would surely have seen the culmination, if not the apotheosis, of his work in Ellis's when the latter concludes (1990:144, 145) that "advances in molecular biological techniques lead to new and powerful approaches. As foreseen by criminologists . . . a new [?] era of rigorous biosocial causal investigations is possible for criminology . . . Ignoring or denying the possible genetic bases of racial differences in criminal behavior has not made the differences go away. Their acknowledgement and inclusion in causal investigations could contribute to understanding the causes of crime, which could, in turn, benefit individuals of all races."

It is a pity that neither Wilson, Herrnstein, nor Ellis seem to have read their Lombroso closely enough (or was it *too* closely?), for he was not to be outdone by his successors one hundred years after publication of his *L'homme criminel*. Initially couched in terms of individual differences, Lombroso (as with his later disciples) proceeds to extrapolate to the propensity of whole "racial" groups to criminality and he, too, summons "ethnographic" evidence ("A French Army Surgeon"). In a later work (1896) entitled "A History of Progress in Criminal Anthropology and Sociology During the Years 1895–1896," Lombroso wrote on the Dinka people of the

Sudan, comparing them, as an "inferior group", to criminals in his own "civilized" society. He avers that "their nose . . . is not only flattened, but trilobed, resembling that of monkeys," thereby placing the Dinka on a lower evolutionary level than himself. As part of his scientific method, then, Lombroso found it necessary to venture "into ethnology to identify criminality as normal behavior among inferior peoples" (Gould 1981:125).

Unfortunately for everyone from Lombroso to our current crop of race-and-crime theorists, the *real* ethnographic evidence on (for example) rates of homicide would reverse their racial hierarchy of propensities towards violence. In one of the few and sadly neglected studies of homicide and suicide in Africa, among twenty-three Ugandan peoples for the period 1945–1954, the average homicide rate was 5.5 homicides per 100,000 person-years (mode, 4.0–6.0; Southall 1960:228; cf. Bohannan 1960a,b:237). In 1972, the crude comparable U.S. rate was 9.2 per 100,000 population. However, as Lee (1979:398) argues, if the population bases of the United States and Vietnam at the time were added (210 million and 30 million respectively), the homicide rate for the United States would be over 100 per 100,000 population. Such a gross comparison is legitimate, since the African figures represent *all* killings during the period assessed.

Lombroso's evolutionary theory of criminal atavism, then, is *directly analogous* to the r/K selection theory applied to the criminality of different human "races" in the late twentieth century by Ellis, Whitney, Rushton, Bogaert, James Q. Wilson, Herrnstein, and Jensen, not to mention their acolyte, George F. Will. The direct parallel between the work of these latter-day scientists and the Gobineau–Lombroso epoch is strengthened by several other similarities in their arguments. Amongst these, perhaps the most important is that they share a commitment to a direct association between race, cranial capacity, intelligence, criminality, unrestrained sexuality, and general cultural inferiority–superiority, however these may be measured. Lombroso believed that criminals had, on average, smaller brains than "upright gentlemen," although his own figures contradicted this contention (Gould 1981:130–2; compare Rushton 1988:1010).

It is interesting to note that James Q. Wilson, as we have seen, promotes the idea that the "folk culture of urban blacks [is] admiring of semiritualistic insult, sly tricksters, and masculine display" (1991:36) and Lombroso, more than one hundred years before, claims that among the stigmata of criminals is that they have their own language, "like the speech of children and savages," and to which "atavism contributes . . . more than anything else. They speak differently; they speak as savages because they are true savages in the midst of our brilliant European civilization" (Lombroso 1887:476, quoted in Gould 1981:132). And the alleged "r-selected unrestrained sexuality" of Africans and African Americans (Rushton and Bogaert 1987 *et passim*) is there in Gobineau: "The animalistic character [of a black man] etched in his loins imposes his destiny from the minute of conception. His fate holds him within the most limited intellectual scope . . . he is possessed, by his desire and also by his will, of an often terrible intensity" (Gobineau 1967:205–6).

It seems that the "terrible intensity" that *we* must explain lies in the relentless pursuit of these racist studies by these selected contemporary Western intellectuals. And the question must yet again be raised: *if* the biological sciences, and especially the study of genetics, have made such enormous advances in the last one hundred to one hundred and fifty or so years since Gobineau and Lombroso, not to mention Broca, Agassiz, Morton, Courtet de l'Isle, Lamartine, Hyppolyte Taine, and numerous others (Cohen 1988; Gould 1981), why is there such an alarming identity between their propositions and those of our contemporary scientific colleagues? The answers to this question are manifold; among the more important are the following.

First, as Walda Katz and Irving Wainer reminded us (1982:32), "Today at least some elements of the U.S. capitalist class are in much the same position as the slave holders were in the 1830s. Faced with a growing opposition to their policies, they are beginning to call upon racist theories in the guise of science to justify increased repression. And, like the 1830s, some scientists are rallying to their defense."

Second, all of our protagonists, both nineteenth-century and late twentieth-century, are ostensibly committed followers of the eighteenth-century European Enlightenment which, we are enthusiastically informed by James Q. Wilson (1991:3), "was brought to the cutting edge of philosophical discourse in the nineteenth and swept everything before it in the twentieth." As such, their arguments must appear to be consistent with rationality and scientific method and, hence, be based upon "evidence."

The concept of "race," nevertheless, is, as we have seen, an *a priori* construction, generated by specific historical and politico-economic forces (see Part II below), which demand a rationalizing ideology. But more than this, the ideology is then *used* as an analytical category to adduce genetic differences between three (or more) "races," which are then supposed to carry enormous causal force in "explaining" the very historical and social conditions that gave rise to the race concept in the first place. The circularity of this performance is clear, but its tautological construction is either hidden or ignored by its champions. Gould's categorization of Lombroso's position readily applies to his late twentieth-century successors (Gould 1981:12): "Lombroso constructed virtually all his arguments in a manner that precluded their defeat, thus making them scientifically vacuous. He cited copious numerical data to lend an air of objectivity to his work."

Third, there is a strong intellectual continuity between the ideas of nineteenth-century scientific racists, the heroes and founding fathers of modern Western liberal democracy, and the contemporary clamor of assertions about the transcendental virtues of bourgeois capitalism. Tocqueville, for example, while a vacillating abolitionist of slavery, was a close friend of Gobineau's. He did not subscribe fully to Gobineau's racial doctrines, but he did not attempt to refute them either. In his *Democracy in America*, he (rather obscurely) blamed slavery and white racism for the condition of blacks in America, but he criticized Gobineau not upon the grounds that his racist theories were wrong, but that they were "untimely" in a political sense (Cohen 1980:198–9). And while James Q. Wilson praises Jefferson, Paine, and Franklin as the American "apostles" of the Enlightenment (1991:3), Gould (1981:32) reminds us that both Franklin and Jefferson "embraced racial attitudes," the former on cultural grounds, the latter subscribing to the notion of the biological inferiority of Africans.

Finally, as I have already noted, racist ideas are not haphazard, individual preferences that come "naturally." They constitute a systematic and false ideology masquerading as "scientific" knowledge that constantly needs updating *by* "*scientists*." In his critique of Jensen, Flynn states (1980:5–6):

> Racism has never been (and can never be) simply a set of ejaculatory utterances, a complex of emotions, or an aesthetic quirk about certain colors. It is a full-blown ideology which asserts empirical hypotheses at every turn . . . The racist not only asserts a connection between race

or color and personal traits; he also asserts that the connection is genetic rather than environmental and he associates a genetic connection with something that is necessary or permanent [you cannot, after all, reverse evolution?]. First, his psychology demands it: his hatred of blacks is such that he does not want to allow for the possibility of redemption and he fears that environmentalism will offer the "inferior" individual a chance of such. Second, the core of his ideology is warning an audience of a threat and the *pollution of the genetic pool* is irreplaceable in its rhetorical impact. Third, there is a claim to his intellectual eminence, that only he really understands history. *Unless the connection between race and culture has remained constant, at least for the duration of historical* time and unless that connection is causal, the causal lines running from race to culture rather than the reverse, history becomes a complex interaction of peoples and cultures, and race loses its explanatory force. This means something the racist cannot tolerate: his kind of history becomes too much like anyone else's history and has nothing unique to contribute (emphasis added).

Anthropologists would do well to take note of and explore Flynn's point about "pollution" in this formulation. And we need also to investigate why and how people like Whitney (1990:140) can quote, accurately to boot, an African American intellectual (Sowell 1983) in support of the idea that "racial differentiation" has been central to human affairs on a global scale, "throughout history," thereby bestowing a primordiality (and hence "naturalism") on the race concept and racism that is patently invalid and prevents any interrogation of their historical provenance and their specific functions. Sowell plays into the hands of the racists by opening his book with the false statement that "Race has affected all kinds of human relationships for thousands of years, and in all parts of the world," and by phrasing his topics in such terms that Whitney can even recruit him in support of the "hierarchy" of races "with the order of black–white–Oriental" (Sowell 1983:15,19; Whitney 1990:140; cf. "Preface," and "Introduction" above and Snowden 1983).

To conclude my argument in this first part of the present work, I will add the proposition that it is *only* in social formations in which knowledge is trapped by assumptions of the autonomous individual subject so characteristic of bourgeois capitalism that such a scientistic racism and the devaluation (indeed, the total displacement) of the "Black Other" can come about (Pandian 1985:70–84). Fully dialectical forms of knowledge, exemplified in non-capitalist societies, simply cannot produce such deformed and alienated kinds of subject-formation.

It is thus anthropology's task not to "repatriate" its already distorted views of "the Other" in order to scrutinize Western bourgeois culture through its alienated gaze, but to expose the mythological and ideological systems upon which such forms of pseudo-knowledge as those discussed so far rest. It must undermine the very *concepts* of race and racism, classism, and sexism that lie at the very foundations of "western civilization" (Appiah 1992; Diamond 1974; Gailey 1992).

I now proceed to a more thorough investigation of the political, economic, social, and epistemological issues underlying the tenacity of alienated forms of Western scientific knowledge about Africa and Africans that characterize the bourgeois capitalist *weltanschauung*.

PART TWO

Africa Unchained: Anthropology, Ideology, and Consciousness in Contemporary Praxis

Two parallel crises have arisen recently, one of vital significance for Africa at this particular historical conjuncture, the other contingent, and yet related to the first. Most crucially, as Africa has begun its post-independence struggle towards a true revolution (Davidson 1990), Western capitalist interests have reacted in two ways. Having lost control of the disintegrating bourgeois and petit-bourgeois post-colonial regimes, while these regimes themselves are losing control over their national populations, these interests are actively involved in counter-revolutionary efforts aimed at subverting a veritably African and socialist revolution.

Secondly, as a necessary concomitant to hegemonic control over the conditions associated with the first, the image of Africa and Africans in the West has had to be disparaged even further than it has been since the eighteenth century, in order to justify the more subtle forms of neocolonialism. The resurrection of the epithet, the "white man's burden," revives nineteenth-century images of an Africa incapable of looking after itself, and therefore dependent upon "aid" from the West; it is explicitly linked to *control*, such as is exercised through the "structural adjustment" conditionality plans (Cheru 1989:34–44).

In a recent book on Africa written by a prominent Washington journalist, a book highly praised in the Western press, a statement typical of this trend appears (Harden 1990:15): "Africa is the most successful producer of babies in recorded history and the world's least successful producer of food." Somalis are pilloried for wrecking their nation and society when it was, in fact, destroyed by a dictator supported during his final years in power by the United States and the West, in complicity with major U.S. oil companies (Rigby 1993; Cohen 1993). Angola is re-embroiled in a catastrophic struggle instigated by a puppet leader, Jonas Savimbi, whose powers were created and are still supported by the C.I.A., and the legitimately elected President of Haiti is labelled as a psychopath when he is overthrown by mass murderers trained and supported by the C.I.A. and the United States military. Both before and after the coup against President Aristide of 1991, the C.I.A. promoted rumours that he was "obstructionist," "difficult," and "paranoid"; and they released a "report" to substantiate these allegations (Farmer 1994:219).

These two processes – enforced economic control and exploitation from outside and the reconstitution of a racist image of a backward, "primitive," dependent Africa and African diaspora preoccupied with what is called in the popular press "grisly tribal wars with atrocities on both sides" – are intimately linked. The product of this synthesis is then used to justify continuing U.S. militarist interventions under the guise of a "new world order" (Amin 1992). I say "reconstitution," since the very idea of a pre-colonial Africa fraught with indigenously generated wars among "savage tribes" is historically and dialectically related to the notion of a presently disintegrating continent divided on "ethnic" or "tribal" lines (see Appendix I). Both are colonial as well as anthropological inventions of a mythical and erroneous past as well as a mis-represented present. The persistence of these images is as integral to the reproduction of neocolonial dominance and the reproduction of international capital as are the images of an "inferior" African race discussed in Part I.

In other words, the racist dogmas of the nineteenth century and earlier that were used to reduce Africa and Africans to a subjugated and permanently dependent status as providers of the labor and wealth of "civilized" ("white") Western nations have reappeared in new and subtle forms. Racism as an internal constituent of imperialism, which was the "first stage of capitalism," was itself constitutive of the capitalist mode of production, and remains so. Anthropology played a significant part in the early production (as well as the later criticism) of these discourses of "denigration" (Stocking 1968; Fabian 1983; Pandian 1985; Harrison 1991; etc.) and still does today, albeit in much more ambiguous ways.

It is my intention to expose some of these discourses and processes of domination through a radical reading and critique of contemporary forms, both popular and scholarly, of the *mis*-representation of Africa, a task I have touched upon in relation to the Maasai peoples of East Africa (Rigby 1992a). Such a task is not possible without reference to the rise of global capitalism, imperialism, and neocolonialism, and the resurgence of "scientific racism," the last of which I have already dealt with in some detail.

I conclude with a brief exploration of what African knowledges can add, and have already contributed, to this struggle; but, most importantly, what they can teach the bourgeois West about its own past and future, *not* in the form of a "repatriated" anthropology as "cultural critique" (cf. Marcus and Fischer 1986), but as perhaps a "new" anthropology grounded firmly in a critical, non-Eurocentric episteme and critique of particular forms of knowledge.

CHAPTER FIVE

Funtionalism, Positivism, Bourgeois Science, Slavery, and Racism

Over the past few years, a number of truly significant theoretical and methodological upheavals have beset anthropology. There is nothing particularly new in this; such "reinventions" and "experimental moments" (Hymes 1969; Marcus and Fischer 1986) have occurred throughout the history of the discipline. What is important about the present crisis is that the very *raison d'être* of anthropology, at least in some places, is in jeopardy. Some anthropologists and observers of anthropologists are more optimistic than others in this debate on anthropology's viability, or even the desirability of its survival. For me, at any rate, certain forms of anthropological practice and discourse still extant should decidedly *not* persist, for they are positively dangerous. For example, Hallpike's disastrous *magnum opus, The Foundations of Primitive Thought* (1979) is a case in point, and is the kind of work non-anthropologists like to take up in their strenuous efforts to justify bourgeois Western intellectual hegemony (e.g. LePan 1989).

But this book, as we have already seen, is not only about the birth, life, and possible death of anthropology, even in its "Africanist" guise. The first two phases in its life cycle, at least, have received extensive attention in numerous works (e.g. Evans-Pritchard 1981; Stocking 1968; Mafeje 1976; etc.). The demise of anthropology has also been the subject of considerable comment and speculation over the years and from a wide variety of viewpoints (e.g. Amin 1980:36–45; Barrett 1984:211–44; Fabian 1983; Mafeje 1976; Rigby 1985:3–4, *et passim*; Stoller 1989; Willis 1969; Fox 1991; etc.). My concern, rather, is that failure of anthropology to confront certain crucial contemporary issues of race, class, and gender, some of which have already been discussed. If anthropology's claims to be the "science of man" are to be taken seriously (even in this sexist English version), this dereliction constitutes a fundamental evasion of responsibility.

While it is freely admitted that anthropology is facing a "crisis of representation," it is insufficiently recognized that its habitual *mis*-representations have profound political, economic, and social (as well as epistemological) effects and consequences (e.g. Amselle and M'bokolo 1985; Southall 1985). Reflecting recently upon the future of anthropology, Barrett comments (1984:220–1): "To expect anthropology to focus on the major expressions of inequality is to request a fundamental shift in the direction of the discipline, for it has rarely done so in the past. Anthropology was the discipline that dealt with colonial societies, and thus should have pioneered the analysis of colonialism. Yet it failed to meet the challenge."

Such criticisms have been expressed for some time, and to repeat them may seem too much like flogging an already proverbially dead horse. Yet the *solutions* to these problems proposed even by radical anthropologists frequently take the form either of changing its object, or replacing its subject, or both. By this I mean, for example, that although most anthropologists (with notable exceptions) would no longer define their discipline's object as "the primitive," opening the path to the study of "complex" and "urban-industrial" societies, they fail to question the epistemological implications of defining their discipline solely by its *object,* even if this object is now more encompassing (Auge 1982 [1979]; Fabian 1983; Kuper 1988).

Again, during a penetrating exposé and critique of racist skeletons in the anthropological closet, Willis not only claims urban ethnography as "one crucial proving ground for [a] new kind of anthropology" in the United States, he also rightly sees that "there is an immediate need to develop active and creative programs to recruit, train, and employ more young black and other colored anthropologists," which in itself is admirable. Yet the epistemological break that would be required for a "new anthropology" is transposed by Willis to methodologically quantitative and contingent terms (1969:147):

> If these programs are successful, then the new colored anthropologists will become articulated with the ghetto poor. They will not be so isolated in white academia as the few colored anthropologists of the past and therefore not as *derivative in their anthropology.* The numerical

increase and the new articulation will encourage colored anthropologists *to initiate distinctive approaches* (emphasis added).

Needless to say, neither the accelerated recruitment programs for black and other "minority" anthropologists, nor the envisaged decline in the derivative nature of mainstream urban anthropology, has come about in the more than twenty-five years since Willis's proposals were made. In any case, neither merely substituting the "urban" for the "primitive," nor replacing white with black inquiring subjects ensures a discipline's epistemological trans-formation or its commitment to radical political alternatives, any more than replacing a colonial (white) bourgeoisie with a local (black) one ensures the liberation of oppressed peoples, as Ngugi wa Thiong'o's and other radical writer's works have often reminded us (e.g. Ngugi 1981, 1986, *et passim*). If colonialist and racist historiography in Africa cannot be successfully defeated with merely ideological weapons, which are often themselves derived from the oppressor's ideological inventory (Temu and Swai 1981; Jewsiewicki and Newbury 1986), anthropology certainly cannot be transformed by such substitutions.

While not abandoning the historical and strategic necessity for ideological confrontation, the position I have adopted and attempt to elaborate here has its roots much more clearly in the prescient position elaborated by Asad in 1973 (Asad 1973:18):

> I believe it is a mistake to view social anthropology in the colonial era as primarily an aid to colonial administration, or as a simple reflection of colonial ideology. I say this not because I subscribe to the anthropological establishment's comfortable view of itself, but because bourgeois consciousness, of which social anthropology is merely one fragment, has always contained within itself profound contradictions and ambiguities – and therefore the potentialities for transcending itself.

Anthropology was a "child of imperialism"; but it was not the *only* child of imperialism, since the very capitalist mode of production itself was such a child; and imperialism, too, had parents. The now castigated dominance of functionalism, for so long and in so many forms of anthropology, was an imperative for the intellectual component in the reproduction of bourgeois capitalist society, as necessary for the "center" as for the "periph-ery." As Mafeje cogently expresses it (1976:311):

In its paradigmatic form functionalism is a product of nineteenth
century Western European bourgeois society, and was never limited
to a single discipline called "anthropology." On the contrary, it
straddled all the life sciences. Analogies from the physical and
biological sciences had been employed in previous centuries to explain
complex self-regulating systems. But their rationalist utilitarian version
was a reflection of the logic of the industrial revolution in England
and France. It is no accident that the founders of modern functionalism,
Auguste Comte and Herbert Spencer, came from France and England.
During their time, rationality, utility or functional value, order and
progress, were guiding principles of bourgeois society. These were both
an affirmation of its achievement and a justification of its continued
existence.

And, we may add, are still so in the ever-changing forms taken by
the reproduction of global capitalism (Amin 1992).

Despite their ostensibly "anti-evolutionist stance," the roots of
functionalist theory lie firmly in the evolutionism of the nineteenth
century and the rationalist justification of the imperialist and
consequently racist expansionism entailed by the rise, growth, and
reproduction of capitalism. Durkheim's functionalism, in fact, did
not prevent him from espousing a biological determinist theory
of criminality which would delight the contemporary proponents
of the racist approach to criminal behavior discussed in the
previous section. Taylor, Walton, and Young (1978:214–15) make
an illuminating comparison between Durkheim and Marx on
crime:

> For Durkheim both crime and the division of labor were normal: both
> of them external social facts . . . In Durkheim's ideal society, organized
> as a spontaneous system of occupational associations and relationships
> of production appropriate to individual aptitudes, crime and deviance
> would not be abolished: they would be expressions of the biological
> inequality of bodily endowments and individual receptivity to
> socialization into the spontaneous social order. For Marx, the division
> of labor and, therefore, crime, are not inevitable or normal, and he
> explicitly denies the utility of looking at individual differences (e.g. of
> will, but equally, implicitly, of biological endowments) in a situation
> where any kind of division of labor still obtains.

We are often correctly told by both French and British
anthropologists of eminence that anthropology was also the child
(legitimate or illegitimate) of the European Enlightenment. What

is seldom added is that the Enlightenment was profoundly bourgeois and that "it sought to make its own anthropological viewpoint universal" (Mafeje 1976:310). The "Eurocentric" discourses produced by these developments, "universalized" not by their explanatory power but through their political, military, and hegemonic domination, are Eurocentric only in a historically contingent and general sense. They are much more explicitly the product of the Euro-American ruling class, the bourgeoisie, and express the interests of this class. Throughout this period and, as we have seen, until the present, the notion of an autonomous, capitalist, "natural" man has also been based upon the crime of an invidious denunciation of an "inferior, Black, Other" (cf. Pandian 1985). The "civilizing mission" and its attendant racism which was the overt characterization of nineteenth-century European imperialism, as was the "manifest destiny" in its American version, was, of course, a *rationalization* for genocide, plunder, economic exploitation, and political repression in the colonies.

As Sartre has so powerfully elucidated, violence inheres in the very *structure* of bourgeois society and colonialism; but it has constantly to be reinvented and put into practice as a process, and racism has been constitutive of this process for the past five hundred years or so (see Fields 1990). Violent people must constantly carry out the violence inhering in the "practico-inert" of structures. Joseph Catalano, commenting upon Sartre's *Critique of Dialectical Reason*, succinctly argues (1986:240), "Sartre's point here is that colonization arises out of the practico-inert violent background of bourgeois, capitalist society, yet transcends this violence in acts of extreme exploitation. Once established, these acts of superexploitation create a new practico-inert, with conditions of even more intense violence. But these conditions *must constantly be recreated and sustained by the colonialists*" (original emphasis).

Even more strongly, this dialectic of violence displaces it on to "the Other," whether colonized Africans or internally marginalized groups. This is precisely the point made by W.E.B. Du Bois in *Black Reconstruction in America, 1869–1880* (1962), where the superexploitation of the Black worker in the U.S. is indelibly established for that period. Manning Marable's brilliant analysis (1983) shows that the situation is similar for African Americans today to what it was in the late nineteenth century, despite cosmetic changes to the structures of contemporary bourgeois society.

All of this has enormous implications for how whites (particularly males), both as European colonialists in Africa and as Americans, throughout this history, totally distort the dialectic of their *own* identity by mis-representing, and thus disparaging, the "Other." As Sartre, with great acuity, indicates (1976:720):

> The colonialist discovers in the [colonized] not only the Other-than-man but also his sworn Enemy (in other words, The Enemy of Man). This discovery does not presuppose resistance (open or clandestine), or riots, or threats of revolt: the violence of the colonialist emerges as an indefinite necessity or, to put it another way, the colonialist reveals the violence of the [colonized], even in his passivity, as the obvious consequence of his own violence and its sole justification. This discovery is made through hatred and fear . . . as a permanent danger which has to be avoided or prevented.

That this hatred and fear was characteristic of bourgeois society in the nineteenth century has been deftly exposed by Peter Gay (1993); in fact, as we have seen, precisely for the period with which our contemporary racist theorists are so enamored! But Sartre continues (1976:720), "Racism has to become a practice: it is not contemplation awakening the significations engraved on things; it is *in itself* self-justifying violence: violence presenting itself as induced violence, counter-violence and legitimate defence."

Substitute in these passages "white" for "colonialist" and "black" for "native" (or colonized), and they apply *pari passu* to the United States and the bourgeois West generally (cf. Césaire 1972). And, with similar substitutions, Sartre's conclusion harks back again to our discussion in Part I above (Sartre 1976:721), "The activity of racism is a *praxis* illuminated by a 'theory' ('biological,' 'social,' or empirical racism, it does not matter which) aiming to keep the masses in a state of molecular aggregation, and to use every possible means to increase the 'sub-humanity' of the natives." Among these possible means, as I have shown, are particular forms of white bourgeois intellectual practice.

In fact, the direct connections between the ideological justifications for nineteenth-century British and French colonialist expansion and the problem of controlling the working class in metropolitan Britain and France were clearly expressed in the

popular and scholarly literature of the time. Sir Richard Burton's
racist attitudes towards Africans were quite explicitly associated
with his plan that they should be perpetual laborers for the white
capitalist class in their glorious Garden of Eden (Burton 1967
[1876]: 311): "I unhesitatingly assert – and all unprejudiced
travellers will agree with me – that the world still wants the black
hand. Enormous tropical regions yet await the clearing and
draining operations by the lower races, which will fit them to
become the dwelling places of civilized men" [quoted in
Brantlinger 1988: 183].

Burton's racism is associated with his class position in England
(Brantlinger locates him as a "marginal aristocrat"), as are the
similarly virulent prejudices of a typical bourgeois, Sir Samuel
Baker; and they can be ascribed to the same cause: the colonial
context. It is imperialism and colonialism that generate a
conviction of racist white superiority that transcends class lines,
not the other way round. And Brantlinger rightly concludes that
the racist *Anchauung* of Baker and Burton "expresses a nostalgia
for a lost authority and a pliable, completely subordinate proletariat
that is one of the central fantasies of imperialism. For opposite
reasons, that fantasy also appealed to explorers from working-class
backgrounds, such as Livingstone and Stanley, whose subordinate
statuses at home were reversed abroad" (Brantlinger 1988:183).

The contemporary power and relevance of such historical
investigations into the construction of racist categories in the
United States is brilliantly explored by Barbara Fields. She notes
(1990:106):

> Race as a coherent ideology did not spring into being simultaneously
> with slavery, but took even more time than slavery did to become
> systematic. A commonplace that few stop to examine holds that people
> are more readily oppressed when they are already perceived as inferior
> by nature. The reverse is more to the point. People are more readily
> perceived as inferior by nature when they are already oppressed.

The very instantiation of "race" as a category of discourse and
practice at all is dependent upon specific historical, material,
politico-economic factors related to the ideological justification of
already existing oppression. Fields expands her argument
(1990:101):

Race is not an element of human biology (like breathing oxygen or reproducing sexually); nor is it even an idea (like the speed of light or the value of π) that can be plausibly imagined to have an eternal life of its own. Race is not an idea, but an ideology. It came into existence at a discernible historical moment and is subject to change for similar reasons. The revolutionary bicentennials that Americans have celebrated with such unction – of independence in 1976 and the Constitution in 1989 – can as well serve as the bicentennial of racial ideology . . . Those holding liberty to be inalienable and holding Afro-Americans as slaves were bound to end by holding race to be a self-evident truth.

The further tragedy of this historical genesis of racist ideology is precisely that it was held to be true by slave-holders *as well as abolitionists*, by contemporary conservatives *and* liberals. "Only if *race* is defined an innate and natural prejudice of color does its invocation as a historical explanation do more than repeat the question by way of an answer. And there an insurmountable problem arises: since race is not genetically programmed, racial prejudices cannot be genetically programmed either, but, like race itself, must arise historically" (Fields 1990:101, original emphasis).

Racism continues to exist in the United States and other capitalist as well as "socialist" countries, therefore, because it is historically necessary for the reproduction of these social formations. As Barbara Fields again elegantly concludes (1990:118):

Nothing handed down from the past could keep race alive if we did not constantly reinvent and re-vitalize it to fit our own terrain. If race lives on today, it can do so only because we continue to create and re-create it, and thus continue to need a social vocabulary that will allow us to make sense, not of what our ancestors did then, but what we ourselves choose to do now.

And this applies equally to those who continue to use racist thinking to struggle against racism under the disguise of "revolutionary" practice.

Similarly, "sexism, racism, and class oppression construct and maintain each other, and they do this not once and for all, but over and over again in changing historical contexts" (S. Harding 1989:14). But they are not, as I have noted, reducible to each other; they are not "parallel social structures," as Harding puts it. Class inequalities and gender discrimination are at least amenable to

question and "reform," ranging from revolutionary change
promoted by Marxists to a denial of the existence of class and
gender as social factors, for example, by conservatives in the United
States, with somewhere in the middle notions of amelioration by
"trickle down" (or is it "trickle up"?) effects and "fair employment"
practices.

The question that must be asked, therefore, is not merely: What
was anthropology's role in the late nineteenth and early twentieth
centuries' phase of racist and imperialist ideology, but also: What
is anthropology's role *now* in either promoting or combating racist
thinking and practices? A partial answer is that populist views of
"race" were often strongly supported by the so-called "science" of
anthropology in the earlier period, and by certain trends in the
psychological and biological sciences as well. The tragedy is that
anthropology and these other sciences continue to propagate views
amenable to racist interpretation, by both omission and
commission. Brantlinger beautifully sums up the nineteenth-
century position as follows (1988:184–5):

> The racist views held by Burton and Baker were at least as close to the
> science of their day as the somewhat less negative views of the
> missionaries. Burton, as a member of the Anthropological Society,
> agreed with its founder James Hunt that the Negro race probably
> formed a distinct species. In contrast, most Darwinians held that the
> races of mankind had a common origin and therefore believed in the
> unity of human nature. But Darwinism was only relatively more
> advanced than Hunt's racism. The development of physical anthro-
> pology and ethnology as disciplines concerned with differences among
> races strengthened the stereotypes expressed by explorers and
> missionaries. Evolutionary anthropology often suggested that Africans,
> if not non-human or of a different species, were such an inferior "breed"
> that they might be impervious to "higher influences" (cf. Montagu
> 1974:28–9).

We have already seen in detail how the unholy marriage between
certain forms of evolutionary biology and the social and
psychological sciences still promotes such stereotypes, no longer
in terms of a "great chain of being" but more "technically" in the
language of "r/K reproductive strategies" (Rushton 1988; cf. Part
I above). Although racist ideas and pronouncements acceptable in
eighteenth- and nineteenth-century Europe and the United States
were made in a manner no longer generally possible without risk

of criticism, the mutual reinforcement of popular and "scientific" myths about race continues with claims of even greater scientific rigor. The pre-evolutionary debates between polygenism and monogenism may have ended with Darwin but, as Gould succinctly puts it, the new oxymoron of "scientific racism" came to prominence in the 1850s (Gould 1981:71–2):

> The defence of slavery did not need polygeny. Religion still stood above science for the rationalization of the social order. But the American debate on polygeny may represent the last time that arguments in the scientific mode did not form a first line of defense for the status quo and the unalterable quality of human differences. The Civil War lay just around the corner, but so did 1859 and Darwin's *Origin of Species*. Subsequent arguments for slavery, colonialism, racial differences, class structures, and sex roles would go forth primarily under the banner of science.

We must keep in mind that it is still true that racism, both pre-scientific and scientific, has very definite historical origins (the former from the early eighteenth to early nineteenth centuries; the latter from the mid-nineteenth century to the present) and continues to adapt to new circumstances, and that Africans and people of African descent in Africa and the Diaspora have suffered *most* from it for the past four hundred years or more, even though it is a much more generalized historical phenomenon (San Juan 1992). There is no doubt either that *capitalist* slavery and the persistence of merchant capital in the reproduction of the world system of capital are closely linked to the elaboration and flexibility of racist ideology (Fox-Genovese and Genovese 1983); the continued growth of racism has at least some of its most tenacious roots in the "New World," particularly in the United States and the Caribbean.

David Brion Davis is unequivocal in establishing the historical genesis of racism by making a clear distinction between ancient slavery, or the "ancient/slave mode of production" in Marx's terms, and slavery under capitalism, although he eschews a Marxist analysis (Davis 1984:33–5; cf. Davis 1966:49–50):

> In antiquity, bondage had nothing to do with physiognomy or skin color. It is true that various Greek writers insisted that slavery should be reserved for "barbarians," but they considered Ethiopians as no more barbarous than the fair Scythians of the north. Skin color and

other somatic traits they attributed to the effects of climate and
environment. Although it would appear that the ancients put no
premium on racial purity and were unconcerned with degrees of racial
mixture, we still have much to learn about the changing origins of black
slaves . . . Throughout antiquity, [however], black slaves were an exotic
variety amid massive populations of Asian and European captors.

Snowden confirms this assertion with extensive research, and
concludes (1983:108) that "One point . . . is certain: the onus of
intense color prejudice cannot be placed upon the shoulders of the
ancients. The Christian vision of a world in which 'there is no
question of Greek and Jew, circumcised and uncircumcised,
barbarian, Scythian, slave, freeman,' owes not a little to earlier
views of man in which color prejudice played no significant role"
(see also Snowden 1970).

Although the rise of racism may, as Montagu asserts (1974), be
traceable to the later eighteenth century, it becomes an integral
part of bourgeois ideology mainly in the nineteenth. It is the thesis
of this book that, since racism is constitutive of the capitalist mode
of production, it is still a crucial element, albeit in different forms,
in contemporary bourgeois ideological formulations and related
practices. This has enormous consequences for domestic and
international policies in late capitalist states; and, furthermore, as
a consequence, racism cannot be dispelled by social engineering
and moral exhortation. There is once again an overt convergence
between populist and pseudo-scientific myths that affects *all* "race
relations," but has the worst consequences for the future of Africa
and people of African descent. Anthropology, through the work
of Boas, W.E.B. Du Bois, and their associates at the end of the
nineteenth century, did more to subvert this insidious ideology than
it is doing now. Recently, however, there has been a renewed and
greater commitment to counter-racist praxis in anthropology than
there has been for some time; I return to a discussion of some of
this work.

CHAPTER SIX

Ideology and the Consolidation of Racial Prejudice in "Scientific" Racism

It is perhaps ironic that when racism had become scientistic ideology in the middle of the nineteenth century, both racism and slavery were looked upon as "positive," until Marx and Engels began dismantling the grounds of positivist social theory. Gouldner tells us (1976:11):

> So far as we know, the term "ideology" was first used by Destutt de Tracy . . . in 1797. De Tracy used "ideology" in a eulogistic way, to name and recommend a new science – the science of ideas. This was to be a positive science that would not imply any "first causes"; that would eschew metaphysics; that had a sense of certainty (or of the positive) since "it does not hint of anything doubtful or unknown . . ." As such, "ideology" would provide the intellectual grounding of a new society.

It is this kind of ideology that was enshrined in the French and American revolutions, the United States Constitution, and the Bill of Rights, among other core myths of bourgeois society, and all of which "entailed an accommodation to 'racism' and 'sexism'" (Gouldner 1976:203).

Apart from the notion of ideology, Raymond Williams uses brilliantly a number of English "key words" which characterize the consolidation of bourgeois hegemony in the later eighteenth and the first half of the nineteenth centuries in order to "map" the changes wrought in Western industrial social formations. These words, "industry," "democracy," "class,", "art," and "culture," either came into more general usage or entirely changed their meanings at this time (Williams 1958:xiii–xx; cf. Williams 1977). We do not have to go further to see from whence James Q. Wilson and those scholars who pursue it (see Part I above) got their racist paradigm (explicitly effusive about the nineteenth century; cf. Gay 1993).

By the 1830s, both capitalist slavery and the *ideology* of racism were being couched in the most positive terms in the United States and elsewhere in the capitalist world. Fredrickson (1971:47) established this point unequivocally by quoting from John C. Calhoun's speech before the United States Senate in 1837, when he stated: "I hold that in the present state of civilization, where two races of different origins, and distinguished by color and other physical differences, as well as intellectual [*sic*], are brought together, the relations now existing in the slave holding states between the two, is, instead of an evil, a good – a positive good."

Fredrickson then proceeds to draw an important parallel between the emergence of this "positivist" ideology of racism and its "rationalization" of slavery with the rise of modern forms of conservative ideology in Europe and the United States (1971:47–8). The contradiction between racism/conservatism on the one hand, and the ostensible bourgeois commitment to *liberté, fraternité, égalité* on the other, *demands* a rationalizing ideology that can assume hegemonic power. Following Mannheim's distinction between "traditionalism" ("the emotional and relatively inarticulate tendency to hold on to established and inherited patterns of life") and "conservatism" ("as conscious and reflective from the first, since it arises as a counter movement in conscious opposition to the highly organized, systematic, and 'progressive' movement"), Fredrickson concludes (1971:48):

> This distinction is clearly analogous to one that can be drawn between racial prejudice as an emotional response to an enslaved and [ostensibly] physically distinct group and the early forms of racism as a "conscious and reflective" attempt to develop, in response to egalitarianism, a world view based squarely and explicitly on the idea that whites are unalterably superior to blacks.

There is little reason, then, to believe that a general bourgeois *weltanschauung*, with an integral racism as one of its major ideological supports, has altered much in its functions; on the contrary, there is much evidence to show that, at the end of the twentieth century, it has in fact expanded in depth, scope, and "explanatory power" for the bourgeois imagination to justify contemporary forms of domination and exploitation, both domestically and abroad. The concomitant and growing misrepresentation of Africa and Africans in the contemporary Western press and popular media, such as in the "theorizing" about AIDS (Chirimuuta and Chirimuuta 1989; Patton 1992) and the role of "tribalism" in what are plainly class wars, is paralleled by certain form of "isolationist," functionalist, anthropology and sociology purporting to deal with contemporary African societies as well as the social structures and cultures of African Americans and the peoples of the Caribbean and Latin America (Stinson-Fernandez 1994).

The racist political economy of the AIDS debate needs special attention from anthropologists, but it is too large and complex an issue to deal with here. In the light, however, of such cogent criticisms of anthropological involvement (or more accurately, non-involvement) in AIDS studies in Africa as those made by Barnett and Blaikie (1992:8), I must digress briefly. While anthropologists might like to maintain that their real contribution in this area lies in an "understanding of the world views of people with AIDS and people living in AIDS-affected areas," Chirimuuta and Chirimuuta (1989) and Patton (1992) show clearly that a local-level struggle against AIDS cannot be pursued without a full awareness of the international political economy of racism and neocolonial hegemony.

For example, Paul Farmer's brilliant demonstration (1994:49–50) that an accusation by a peasant from central Haiti, "You know, don't you, that the United States has a trade in Haitian blood," is more than poetic mystification; it is firmly rooted in fact, and demands anthropological attention. Anthropologists working in Africa have an absolute obligation to react when Farmer can note for Haiti (1994:262) that "We should question modes of seeing," not of the peasants themselves, but of the students of AIDS who "depict AIDS as having come *from* Haiti rather than *to* Haiti. All of these notions are expedient, predictable, and quite false. Their success speaks volumes, however, about the power of those who have a stake in perpetuating such chicanery."

CHAPTER SEVEN

The Hegemony of Racist Ideology: Color, Status, and the Economic Basis of Racism

Racial prejudice and stereotyping arose with the expansion of merchant capital and the origins of capitalist slavery, beginning in the fifteenth century; the former continues in the twentieth as a necessary concomitant of the reproduction of global capitalism (Amin 1992; R. Allen 1990). But it is highly significant that the origins and growth of contemporary forms of racism (as well as modern sexism) coincide historically with the maturing of the capitalist mode of production in Europe and the United States in the middle of the nineteenth century. African historical experience, particularly, has been penetrated by racist categories for the entire period.

While the history of anthropology exhibits both racist and anti-racist movements and explanatory frameworks, there have been relatively few attempts by anthropologists to study the persistence of the more hidden racist categories of global culture (including anthropology itself), which are still dominated by white, male, hegemonic interests; and this stricture applies also to ostensibly "socialist" formations such as Cuba. This hiatus is peculiar, given the claims of anthropology to the status of a "holistic" discourse on the human condition in all its forms. It is only recently that this deficit has begun to be made up, for example, by writers such as Harrison (1988, 1991), Blakey (1987, 1991), Baker (1994a, 1994b), Patterson and Spencer (1994), Sacks (1993), Azoulay (1994) and others (see also *Critique of Anthropology*, 12,3, 1992 and 14,2, 1994). I return to consider some of these contributions.

Two major problematics, among others, provide the grounds for a counter-hegemonic and revolutionary anthropological praxis in the struggle against racism and neocolonialism in relation to Africa and the African Diaspora: (a) the growth of anti-imperialist and anti-racist science and philosophy in Africa and the African Diaspora; and (b) the Marxist critique of capitalism, class, and bourgeois culture (e.g. Bates, Mudimbe, and O'Barr 1993; Comaroff and Comaroff 1991; Rigby 1992a,b,c; Van Binsbergen and Geschiere 1985). Neither of these two problematics can be reduced to the other; but a dialectical relation between them makes each much stronger than either can be separately.

In the light of the vast accumulation of anthropological "experience" in Africa, it is incumbent upon anthropology to examine, assess, and expose the insidious forms of race, class, and gender categorizations that permeate every aspect of modern bourgeois global culture. An anthropology that ignores or marginalizes these issues is in danger of supporting the oppressions that are their direct result.

The hegemonic power of racist categories is exposed by their penetration into the discourses of, most particularly, African American, Caribbean, and Latin-American populations of predominantly African descent. Through the history of exploitation and colonialism, it has also affected the construction of contemporary African social formations and their discourses, but in very different forms (Mudimbe-Boyi 1992). Contemporary African discourses *in Africa* concerning the continuing struggle for revolutionary liberation are largely unconcerned about racist categories except, for understandable reasons, among some factions in South Africa; and even there, the African National Congress has always eschewed racist categories in everything from armed struggle to cultural liberation.

In the United States, the Caribbean, and Latin-America, however, it is well known that there are elaborate scales relating to "color" and "status" which have their roots in slavery and still operate as a component in cultural and political discourses and practices. Commenting upon the variety and complexity of these systems of "racial" classification in the Caribbean, Mintz observes (1974:24):

> The population of discernible African origin in the Antilles as a whole
> – a matter always subject to local norms of perception and assortment
> – probably make up at least 75% of the total. The importance and
> meaning of racial identity in these societies varies significantly from

one to another and, to a considerable extent, within the social fabric of each component society. Allowing for all these qualifiers, the fact remains, however, that the Caribbean region is a core area of contemporary Afro-America . . . If we turn from physique to ethnicity and culture, the picture grows yet more complicated and diverse.

These complexities are exacerbated by the continuing neocolonial subjugation of these social formations, and the "internal colonial" status of the majority of African Americans in the United States. But that does *not* mean that the hegemony of bourgeois racist ideology is complete, even in these latter cases: there are strong counter-hegemonic forces gaining strength despite the adoption of the oppressors' categories by some subaltern fractions. For example, Michel-Rolph Trouillot describes succinctly the situation in Haiti (1990:112):

Saint Domingue, and then Haiti, inherited a differential evaluation of races, colors, religions, and cultures. This evaluation included an aesthetic in which blackness was found at the bottom of the scale. To pretend that this aesthetic has disappeared is ludicrous . . . Admittedly, aesthetic evaluations vary according to socio-economic class and phenotype of those who judge, and the results are sometimes surprising to foreigners. Generally speaking "white," for example, is not considered the most pleasing color. Social evaluations of phenotypes in Haiti are nonetheless generally *Western dominated* and, other things being equal, beyond a certain degree of increased melanin, these evaluations imply a denigration of blackness.

The relative *incompleteness* of hegemonic forms, however, allow for the appearance of serious contradictions and, hence, leave room for counter-hegemonic and political struggle. Thus Trouillot continues (1990:112–3):

But here again, other things are rarely equal . . . Thus the reader who is unfamiliar with Haiti must be immediately cautioned lest he or she take the preceding to imply that Haitian color prejudice is simply a toned-down version of Western racism . . . If it is important to note that Haitian color prejudice relates to a Western-dominated hierarchy of races, colors, religions, and cultures, it is equally crucial to note that very few Haitians, even among the elites, *ever accepted that hierarchy as a "true" depiction of their reality* (emphasis added).

Trouillot then proceeds to elaborate upon the forms taken by "cultural guerilla war" in Haiti, the forms of counter-hegemonic struggle. In Africa, on the other hand, Western-imposed racial categories have taken two basic forms. The first postulates, as we have seen, that all Africans, particularly of those social formations called "sub-Saharan," are inferior to all whites, and often to other "races" (such as "Arabs" and "Indians"); the second divides African societies themselves along "racial" lines, and attributes racist attitudes to some African peoples themselves. Both popular mythology and anthropological inquiry have fostered these types of racism; but, perhaps, anthropology has contributed more to the latter kind than to the former.

Some anthropologists may disagree with the main point that I am making – viz, that the *ideology* of racism is the direct result of capitalism and colonialism – as illustrated by Harris's otherwise enlightening discussion of the rise of racial determinism (1968:80–107). But we can also argue that ideologies take on lives of their own, a relative autonomy, and thus have historical effects and consequences. Of course, Harris's discussion would have benefited from Mannheim's distinction, already referred to, between racism as emotional reaction and racism as "rationalist ideology." Walter Rodney phrases it elegantly (1982:88–9):

> Occasionally, it is mistakenly held that Europeans enslaved Africans for racist reasons. European planters and miners enslaved Africans for *economic* reasons, so that their labor power could be exploited. Indeed, it would have been impossible to open up the New World and to use it as constant generator of wealth had it not been for African labor. There was no other alternative: the American (Indian) population was virtually wiped out and Europe's population was too small for settlement overseas at that time. Then, having become utterly dependent on African labor, Europeans abroad found it necessary to rationalize that exploitation in racist terms.

In reference to the United States, Barbara Fields makes an analogous point (1990:99):

> Probably a majority of American historians think of slavery in the United States primarily as a system of race relations – as though the chief business of slavery were the production of white supremacy rather than the production of cotton, sugar, rice, and tobacco. One historian

has gone as far as to call slavery "the ultimate segregator." He does not ask why Europeans seeking the "ultimate" method of segregating Africans would go to the trouble and expense of transporting them across the ocean for that purpose, when they could have achieved the same end so much more simply by leaving the Africans in Africa.

Certainly, most African American and Caribbean historians are not susceptible to these inverted arguments, overturned so effectively by Du Bois and (in 1948) by Cox, and later by Rodney, Fields, and others. Vincent Harding, for example, shows how, as early as the 1820s, an African American freeman called David Walker (born in 1785 in Wilmington, North Carolina) had already articulated the economic motives for slavery and its concomitant racism, then at its "pre-scientific" stage. Walker based his attack on slavery and racism upon a "profound, unshakable, belief in the justice of God," but added (V. Harding 1981:89–90):

> His observations across the land led him to refer again and again to the economic motives behind white oppression. Early in the *Appeal* he said that, after years of observation and reading, "I have come to the immovable conclusion that [the Americans] have, and continue to punish us for nothing else, but for enriching them and their country".

He even commented that, from the beginning of African international contacts with whites, "I do not think that we were natural enemies of each other"; enmity arose with the beginning of the slave trade and the avarice of the whites.

CHAPTER EIGHT

Racist Ideology Inventing History: The "Hamitic Myth" and Rwanda-Burundi

The hegemonic power of racist dogma, so strongly developed in Europe and America, profoundly affected the colonial history of Africa; but it failed to define the parameters of contemporary African revolutionary struggle. Achebe is right when he comments (1989:43):

> Needless to say, we [Africans] do have our own sins and blasphemies recorded against our name. If I were God, I would regard as the very worst our acceptance – for whatever reason – of racial inferiority. It is too late in the day to get worked up about it or to blame others, much as they may deserve such blame and condemnation. What we need to do is to look back and try to find out where we went wrong, where the rain began to beat us.

As I have already mentioned, counter-ideology based upon the invention of our oppressors is a necessary but not sufficient weapon in counter-hegemonic struggle and anti-racist praxis (Appiah 1992,1993), a point to which I return again. But the situation in Africa is complicated by the second form of racism, aided and abetted by anthropology and the hoary old colonial policy of *divide et impera*. A prime example of this in anthropology is the "Hamitic myth" in Eastern African studies, invented in the nineteenth century by Count de Gobineau and first applied to East Africa by adventurer John Hannington Speke in 1865. This myth was later eagerly adopted by anthropologists and historians in the early twentieth century.

Anthropologists continued to use the term "Hamitic" at least until the 1950s, particularly as embodied in the category "Nilo-Hamitic" as used in the International African Institute's *Ethnographic Survey of Africa* (e.g. Huntingford 1953; Gulliver and Gulliver 1953). The Hamitic category was originally perpetrated as a racial myth for political reasons and in the interests of European imperialist designs and colonization and the associated theory of "Negro inferiority." Whites refused to believe that "true Africans" could have a varied, complex, and exciting history; the increasing evidence for such a history had to be "explained" by the intrusion of a "white (Caucasoid) element": the result, the "Hamites."

In 1966 and 1970 respectively, anthropologists Aidan Southall and Archie Mafeje, together with archaeologist Merrick Posnansky (1966), exploded the Hamitic myth; but it continues to be a part of popular mythology in eastern African history. Southall (1966:63) noted that "it is recognized that the adoption of linguistic terms like Bantu, Hamitic, and Nilotic as labels for physical groupings is unsound and grossly misleading." And he added (1966:63, fn.3): "This is particularly true of the term Hamitic, which has no agreed physical or linguistic referent and is a fertile source of misconception. It is most deplorable that these errors should still be perpetrated in what ought to be reliable works such as Seligman's *Races of Africa* (3rd edition) (Oxford 1957)." It has since been shown that the term Hamitic is not even useful in any form of linguistic classification (Ehret 1971).

It is perhaps ironic, but hardly surprising, that while European and American anthropologists and historians continued to use this term until the early 1960s (Oliver and Mathew 1963), African and African American social scientists and historians had dismissed the idea years before. For example, as early as 1946, W.E.B. Du Bois wrote (1981:92):

> What are the peoples who from vague prehistory emerged as the Africans of today? The answer has been bedevilled by the assumption that there was in Africa a "true" Negro and that this pure aboriginal race was mixed with a mythical "Hamitic race" which came apparently neither from Europe, Asia, nor Africa. We may dismiss this "Hamitic" race as a quite unnecessary assumption.

Similarly, from at least 1955 onwards, Cheikh Anta Diop took up the "Hamitic" myth in eastern African history, exposing its racist underpinnings. Commenting upon the "Hamitic" element and its "Nilo-Hamitic" manifestation as claiming a "Caucasoid" factor in the prehistory and history of East Africa, Diop notes (1974:273):

> The theory that makes Caucasoids of the Dinka, Nuer, Masai [sic], etc., is the most unwarranted ... To call a Shilluk, a Dinka, or a Masai a Caucasoid is as devoid of sense and scientific validity for an African as it would be for a European to claim that a Greek or a Latin are [sic] not white. The desperate search for a non-Negro solution [to the problem of who created the ancient and modern civilizations of Black Africa] sometimes leads to talk about "a primitive stock that might not as yet have assumed a differentiated Black or White character," or to whitening Negroes such as the Masai. All the human types found in Kenya from the Palaeolithic to the end of the Neolithic are perfectly distinguishable as Negroes ... [Anthropologists] admit, for example, that from the Palaeolithic to our day Kenya, East Africa, and the Upper Nile have been inhabited by the same population which has remained anthropologically unchanged, with the Masai as one of the most authentic representatives [cf. Rigby 1992a: particularly Ch.3].

What neither Diop nor Du Bois do, however, is to analyse the specific historical conditions for the production of the Hamitic myth as a racist ideology.

The hegemonic power of western racism is so entrenched, however, that it even penetrated Maasai ideas about themselves. Thus in 1980, Tepilit ole Saitoti wrote (1980:20):

> The origins and history of the Maasai are shrouded in mystery and myth. The race [sic] is considered a hybrid between the Nilotes, a people coming from the Nile region,and the Hamites,a people originating in North Africa ... Hamitic practices among the Maasai range from circumcision and clitoridectomy in initiation rites and the age-grade system among young warriors to a dislike of eating fish and a scorn for blacksmiths. The Hamitic Nuer of Sudan also share the Maasai belief that they are the custodians of the earth's cattle.

The confusions here between the concepts of "race," linguistic groups, and cultural practices are understandable, given the enormous anthropological "authority" behind the Hamitic myth. What is missing in some of the critiques of the myth is that it was adapted uncritically by anthropologists from its original racist (Gobineau) and colonialist (Speke) origins.

The most detailed and racist of anthropological elaborations of

the Hamitic myth was produced in 1932 by C.G. and Brenda
Seligman in their survey of southern Sudanese ethnography, *The
Pagan Tribes of the Nilotic Sudan*. In this book, the Seligmans claimed
unambiguously that "the manner of origin of the Negro-Hamitic
people will be understood when it is realized that the incoming
Hamites were pastoral Caucasians, arriving wave after wave, better
armed and of sterner character than the agricultural Negroes."
They continue (1932:4):

> At first the Hamites, or at least their aristocracy, would endeavour to
> marry Hamitic women, but it cannot have been long before a series of
> peoples combining Negro and Hamitic blood arose; these, superior
> to the pure Negro, would be regarded as inferior to the next incoming
> wave of Hamites and be pushed further inland [?] to play the part of
> an incoming aristocracy *vis-á-vis* the Negroes on whom they impinged
> . . . The end result of one series of such combinations is to be seen in
> the Masai [*sic*], the other in the Baganda, while an even more striking
> result is offered by the symbiosis of the Bahima of Ankole and the
> Bahera [*sic*].

It is important to note the provenance the Seligmans' book, *which
was reissued in 1965*, and the influence of its authors, particularly
in British social anthropology but also in anthropology as a whole.
As Kuper tells us (1973:25; cf. Kuklick 1991:50, *et passim*), not only
was C.G. Seligman Malinowski's "patron" at the London School
of Economics, he was also Evans-Pritchard's teacher and mentor.
In fact, Evans-Pritchard later provided some of the ethnographic
materials for the Seligmans' book, which was partly sponsored by
the Rockefeller Research Fund (Seligman and Seligman 1932:xv).
To be fair to Evans-Pritchard, we must note that the Seligmans make
it clear that he "must in no way be held responsible for the
presentation of the facts or our conclusions concerning them"
(1932:xiii).

Such anthropological "theories" masquerading as historical
"facts" are tantamount to making Camelot a core event in English
history, or even believing in the tooth fairy and Santa Claus (Fields
1990:96), and appear with hindsight to be figments of the
anthropologists' imaginations. But the problem is not so simple.

As for Maasai, who seem to be so frequently recruited as
exemplars *par excellence* of the Hamitic myth (and its refutation!),
I have had occasion to demonstrate the colonialist motives behind
attributing "racial" distinctiveness *as well as "racial consciousness"*

to them, for example, in a work published by colonial administrator
Sydney Hinde and his wife Hildegarde (1901:109):

> The Masai are, unquestionably, of far greater interest than most African
> peoples, and the fast approaching extinction of the pure stock is a
> matter to be largely regretted. Although under the conditions of
> European government they would not be allowed to resume their
> lawless raids among the surrounding tribes, the destruction of so virile
> a race would, nevertheless, be a permanent loss to East Africa.

What the Hindes do not mention is that the British colonialists
used Maasai against their neighbors in the process of colonization
(Waller 1976), on which I concluded (Rigby 1992a:28), "What we
have again is the fundamentally racist and contradictory nature of
colonialist conceptions of the history and culture of Africans in
general and Maasai in particular." I also noted that such misrepresentations have their roots in the political economy of
colonialism and continue to have unfortunate political effects for
Maasai in contemporary Kenya and Tanzania.

In a remarkable contribution to Amselle and M'Bokolo's book,
Au coeur de l'ethnie (1985), Chrétien shows how the "Hamitic" myth
became a self-fulfilling political myth of massively destructive and
tragic proportions in colonial and post-colonial Rwanda and
Burundi. The most widely known anthropological work on Rwanda
that is available in English is Jacques Maquet's *The Premise of
Inequality in Rwanda* (1961). Although Maquet explicitly eschews
the "linguistic term 'Hamites'" to describe the Batutsi (1961:12),
he perpetuates what he himself calls "physical or racial stereotypes"
(1971:172–3) by photographing "tall" Batutsi against the sky, and
the "short" Bahutu ("agricultural Negroes") against the ground.

As Southall (1985:570–1) points out in his review of *Au coeur de
l'ethnie*, the Belgian colonialist exaggeration of physical differences
between Bahutu and Batutsi into "racial" categories was a purely
political expedient to divide and rule ("indirectly"!) where different
"tribes" could not easily be invented and set against each other.
This has not prevented the Western press from calling them
separate "tribes" in their reports on post-colonial class struggles
in these countries.

For colonial administrators, missionaries, and local Christian
élites-to-be, the Batutsi were the "best, most intelligent, most
energetic chiefs, best able to understand progress and most

acceptable to the people." So they were given privileges all round, special exclusive educational opportunities to "man the administration at all levels, while Hutu could man the mines and plantations." To this colonial political economy of separation and control was added the notion that "to suppress the Tutsi 'caste' . . . would be the greatest mistake government could make, leading straight to anarchy, communism, and anti-European hatred" (Southall 1985:571).

Furthermore, when tragic conflict arose between Bahutu and Batutsi in the post-colonial states of Rwanda and Burundi, leading to enormous and continuing loss of life and the creation of a major refugee problem in eastern Africa, the strife could be blamed by Western observers upon "primordial," "tribal" antagonisms, exculpating entirely the colonial period, policies, and government. As Southall, following Chrétien, summarizes it (1985:571), "Once the system was established, blame for it could be put upon the Tutsi and Hutu themselves . . . School segregation was blamed on Hutu passivity in contrast to Tutsi brains. When Hutu were let into seminaries, they were indoctrinated with the eternal rightness of their subjugation by religious sanction" (see Appendix 1).

Thus, anthropologists and anthropological categories, while obviously not constituting the sole cause of the tragedy of post-colonial conflict in Africa, have exacerbated and perpetuated "racial/tribal" stereotypes within African populations, and they are *politically responsible* for some of their consequences.

But if these anthropological mythologies of "race" have continuing implications for Africa, the systematic debasement of Africans, African Americans, and all peoples of African descent by the racist pseudo-biological, psychological, medical, and criminological "scholarship" of some Western intellectuals, such as those I have addressed in Part I of this book, are even more dangerous. For we in Africa, at least, can eventually deal with the colonial legacy on our own terms (Appiah 1992), even if we have a long way to go. Racial mythology, created and perpetuated by colonial and post-colonial hegemonic forces, continues to bedevil foreign, bourgeois journalism, social science, medical science, and literature. In fact, there is a strong and distinctive analogy between what Achebe calls "colonialist criticism" (1989:68–96) and some contemporary forms of ethnography, and I must now turn to a brief exploration of this.

CHAPTER NINE

Hobbesian "Realism" and "Taking Responsibility"

While I fully agree with Azoulay (1994:16) that "anthropology should be reclaimed from the current stronghold of literary criticism and cultural studies," since "textuality" and "texts" . . . "do not speak back," I think "anthropologists who treat the subject of race need actively to look for and accommodate a range of perspectives" (Azoulay 1994:23).

For Achebe, "colonialist criticism" is virulently anti-African in that it denies any specificity to African literature and culture by imposing bourgeois morality and norms as if they were universal categories against which anything African must be "measured." Similarly, some contemporary anthropology masquerades as a "tough-minded" description of "reality" in which Western bourgeois concepts and categories are imposed as universal and against which African social formations and institutions can be "assessed" (e.g. Ensminger 1992; cf. Rigby 1994). Both practices are profoundly anti-historical as well as racist.

In his trenchant exposé of Philip A. Allen's review (1971) of Yambo Ouologuem's novel, *Bound to Violence* (1971), as an "example of sophisticated, even brilliant, colonialist criticism," Achebe finds it necessary to conduct his exercise in counter-critique because, "strange as it may sound, some of its ideas and precepts do exert an influence on our [African] writers, for it is a fact of our contemporary world that Europe's powers of persuasion [hegemony] can be far in excess of the merit and value of her case" (1988:77). Allen sees Ouologuem's novel as basically concerned with the "forcing of moral universality on African civilization." Allen goes on (quoted in Achebe 1989:77–8): "This morality is not only "un-African" – denying the standards set by omnipresent ancestors, the solidarity of communities, the legitimacy of social contract: it is a Hobbesian universe that extends beyond the wilderness, beyond the white man's myths of Africa, into all civilizations, theirs and ours."

Allen's equation of a "Hobbesian universe" with a universalistic morality is entirely inappropriate. Not only does a Hobbesian position represent merely a philosophical gloss upon the transition from absolutism to capitalist bourgeois values, it invokes the earliest and crudest forms of this ideology. As Marx notes (1954:368, n.2), "On the whole . . . the early English economists sided with Bacon and Hobbes as their philosophers; while at a later period, the philosopher [*par excellence*] of political economy in England, France, and Italy was Locke." But for Allen, this "Hobbesian universe" not only posits a "universal reality" (and "morality"), it also necessarily eschews a political commitment to an African liberation in literature and life.

Allen then compounds his philosophical insularity by trying to show that Ouologuem avoids local African models by giving us "an Africa cured of the pathetic obsession with racial and cultural confrontation and freed from invidious tradition-mongering." The conflicts of *Bound to Violence* are, for Allen, "those of the universe, not accidents of history." Presumably, for Mr Allen, Hobbes himself does not qualify as an "accident of history," but reveals himself as a purveyor of "universal truths" which go beyond the issues of human liberation. For, Allen informs us, "Ouologuem does not accept Fanon's idea of liberation, and he calls African unity a theory for dreamers. His Nakem is no more the Mali of Modibo Keita or the continent of Nkrumah than the golden peace of Emperor Sundiata or a moral parish of Muntu."

Achebe proceeds to draw our attention to Allen's "significant antithesis between the infinite space of 'a Hobbesian universe' and 'the moral parish of Muntu' with its claustrophobic implications"; and he asks with pertinent forcefulness, "Who but Western Man could contrive such arrogance?" (Achebe 1989:78–9).

Allen's Eurocentrism posing as universalism is the literary and aesthetic equivalent of James Q. Wilson's (as well as Jensen *et al.*'s) appeal to "science" as a final, universal, arbiter for the validity of their work. I have, in Part I, already dealt with Rushton, Whitney, Ellis, and company on these issues and the pseudo-science behind them; there is no need for further comment here, save to indicate the analogy. Allen's invocation of Hobbes is not an accident, even if it is tinged with philosophical ignorance. This brings us squarely back to some forms of contemporary anthropology in which (neo-?) neo-Darwinist influences are resurgent.

Although Marx and Engels were impressed with certain lessons that could be drawn from Darwin's work, they long ago discerned the influences of bourgeois thought upon his ideas. In a letter to Engels of 18 June 1862 (Darwin's *Origin of Species* had been published in 1859), Marx wrote, "It is remarkable how Darwin recognizes among beasts and plants his English society with its division of labor, competition, opening up of new markets, 'invention,' and the Malthusian 'struggle for existence.' It is Hobbes's *bellum omnium contra omnes* . . ." (Marx and Engels, 1862; quoted in Schmidt 1971:46).

And in 1875, Engels wrote to P.C. Lavrov (Marx and Engels 1970:478): "The whole Darwinist teaching of the struggle for existence is simply a transference from society to nature of Hobbes's doctrine of *bellum omnium contra omnes* and of the bourgeois-economic doctrine of competition together with Malthus's theory of population."

This brings us back again to the present prominence in both anthropology and the popular imagination of biological reductionism. But I must examine further the current development of what could accurately be called the cultural and social anthropological version of "colonialist criticism."

Achebe acutely observes (1989:79), "Running through Mr. Allen's review is the overriding thesis that Ouologuem has somehow restored dignity to his people and their history by investing them with responsibility for violence and evil . . . And we are to understand, by fairly clear implication, that this is something brave and new for Africa, this manly assumption of responsibility."

The problem with this, apart from Allen's patronizing attitudes, is that, as Achebe puts it (1989:79), "a good deal of colonialist rhetoric always turned on that very question. The moral inferiority of colonized peoples, of which subjugation was a prime consequence and penalty, was most clearly demonstrated in their unwillingness to assume roles of responsibility."

This view, combined with an insistence upon the *cultural inferiority* of African societies, engendered by virulent (and often hidden) forms of cultural imperialism, has consequences disastrous for Africans and peoples of African descent, and must provide a focus for counter-hegemonic struggle for cultural liberation. As Achebe perceptively continues (1989:79):

> Now, to tell a man that he is incapable of assuming responsibility for himself and his actions is of course the utmost insult, to avoid which some Africans will go to any length, will throw anything into the deal; they will agree, for instance, to ignore the presence of the role of racism in African history or pretend that somehow it was all the black man's own fault.

There is a haunting parallel between what may be seen as Ouologuem's inadvertent *mea culpa* and the contemporary role of neo-conservative African American intellectuals. Just as James Q. Wilson and Glayde Whitney detach criminality from socio-economic and political processes and forces, leaving only a genetic explanation for high crime rates among Blacks in the United States, so too do neo-conservative Black intellectuals curry favor with white America. As Derrick Bell, referring to Thomas Sowell's work (1984), notes for the United States (1987:14), "Today, as policy makers seek to abandon civil rights enforcement, certain experts assert that the plight of blacks is the fault of blacks or the social programs on which the poor rely. When such claims are expounded by blacks, they obtain a certain deceptive authority."

Bell continues, "Such blacks, knowingly or unknowingly, dispense a product that fills the present national need for outrageous anti-black comment. Many whites welcome it. Black neo-conservatives, as some of these black critics describe themselves, gain wide recognition for their views" (ibid.). White delight with Black neo-conservatives is abundantly confirmed by such as Glayde Whitney (1990:140) in his excursus into the essentiality of "race" differences and the racial determination of criminality when he invokes Sowell's (1984) work in support of his assertion that, "Worldwide and throughout history a racial differentiation with an order of black–white–oriental has tended to be persistent for many behaviorally based characteristics."

Not only do such ridiculous assertions and admissions of guilt ignore the role of racism in global and African (and African American) history; they *ignore history* itself (Gilroy 1993; San Juan 1992). The politico-economic and anthropological versions of cultural and racial oppression operate upon several levels simultaneously. They are, in Althusserian (and Freudian) terms, "overdetermined." Current at the broadest level now is the general idea that Africans cannot properly govern and look after themselves, since, through their "primitive" agricultural practices and social institutions, they are constantly beset by famines and other disasters which require external ("Western") aid to ameliorate. The historical dimensions of pre-colonial, colonial, and post-colonial political economy in the creation of famine conditions are ignored, and the misplaced zeal of current international solutions is brushed under the discursive carpet (*Review of African Political Economy*, No. 45. 1988; cf. Franke and Chasin 1980).

CHAPTER TEN

The Africanist "Heart of Darkness"

Before I return to the issues specifically of anthropology, Africa, and racism, a recent event in the United States media allows me to digress briefly to a consideration of Christopher Miller's excellent *Blank Darkness* (1985). In December 1993, a newly made-for-cable television movie of Joseph Conrad's *Heart of Darkness* was aired on Home Box Office, ostensibly because this novel, first published in 1899, is a "classic" of the English literary canon and presumably one which deals with "universal" themes.

Miller sees this novel as a continuation of the classical tradition in European literature and art, for example, in France, ranging from Baudelaire and Rimbaud to Sade and Céline. After an epigram by anthropologist Leo Frobenius ("Beside [Asia], Africa looks like a shapeless, uncouth giant. A flat cake, vast and amorphous"), Miller notes (1985:6), "Utterances on Africa tend to be hints rather than statements, hearsay rather than direct evidence, allegory rather than realism." How apposite this is to current journalism and the mis-representation of our continent! Miller begins his chapter on Conrad as follows (1985:169):

> If Africanist discourse had not existed prior to the advent of the modern novel, one would have had to invent it. There is a "blank" in the science of narrating that can be filled with any figure one likes and that "Africa" has been made to fill with its emptiness. That coincidence, between a place in the interpretation of literature and a place supposedly in the world, is the object of the last part of this study . . . The pattern exists outside of what we consider narrative (in poetry and the graphic arts) and vice versa. There are thus two questions to be differentiated. First, what is the place, the blank in any narrative that a figure such as "Africa" is eligible to fill? Second, what happens to the figure of Africa when it is inserted in a narrative scheme?

Miller's intriguing answer to these questions is that "Africanist narration," including this novel and some anthropology, represents narration not merely deprived of historicity, but in effect, in reverse: narration "backwards." This is how he puts it (Miller 1985:171–2):

> [*Heart of Darkness*'s] most basic armature – the phrase "travelling back" – [is] a paradigm of Africanist narration. Whereas the pre-anthropologists (such as de Brosses) and the "ethnologists" (such as Gobineau) . . . depicted the primitive world as static and isolated, the project of narration as seen in [*Heart of Darkness*] will be to reach back to that frozen past and make it real in writing. Travelling back means bringing the primitive world forward, or, more accurately, projecting the primitive world as an anteriority that can be reached geographically . . . Narration, which would normally be the recounting of sequential events (a model from which it can never wholly escape if only because one word, one paragraph, must follow another), is here literally a "backwards" process. As V.S. Naipaul writes in *A Bend in the River*, the strongest Africanist narration since *Heart of Darkness*: "I am going in the wrong direction."

Perhaps needless to say, Naipaul represents the epitome of contemporary colonialist discourse (Achebe calls him "this modern Conrad," 1989:28) parroted by an ex-colonial subject, and his critical writing is an excellent example of subaltern "colonialist criticism." But Conrad's almost psychotic racism is revealed by Achebe (1989:6–7): "Having shown us Africa in the mass, Conrad then zeros in . . . on a specific example, giving us one of his rare descriptions of an African who is not just limbs or rolling eyes:

> And between whiles I had to look after the savage who was fireman. He was an improved specimen; he could fire up a vertical boiler. He was there below me, and, upon my word, to look at him was as edifying as seeing a dog in a parody of breeches and a feather hat, walking on his hind legs. A few months of training had done for that really fine chap. He squinted at the steam gauge and at the water gauge with an evident effort of intrepidity – and he has filed his teeth too, the poor devil, and the wool of his pate shaved into queer patterns, and three ornamental scars on each of his cheeks. He ought to have been clapping his hands and stamping his feet on the bank, instead of which he was hard at work, a thrall to strange witchcraft, full of improving knowledge.

And Achebe concludes, "As everybody knows, Conrad is a romantic on the side. He might not exactly admire savages clapping their hands and stamping their feet but at least they have the merit of being in their place, unlike this dog in parody breeches. For Conrad, things being in their place is of the utmost importance."

And the "place" is, of course, both specific in time and space: the remote past, and in "savage" Africa. But the construction of a mythical past *for* Africa from, as it were, an external consciousness, is also evident in anthropology. We have seen the case of the "Hamitic myth"; the propensity for backwards narration may also be seen in the classics of functionalist anthropology. For example, in discussing the "value and limitations of history" for the "dynamics of culture change" in Africa, Malinowski embarks on a "search for the zero point of change" (1945:27ff.). He chides Lucy Mair for maintaining that "all the anthropologist could do and should do in the study of culture contact is to compare the traditional Native institutions, i.e., the Native culture at the zero point of contact influences, with the present-day situation" and asserts that "[reconstruction of the pre-colonial past] is and will remain one of the main tasks of scientific ethnology" (1945:28). But, he adds (1945:29), "It is equally important to realize that the 'past remembered' – that is, its vision in man's memory – need not, in fact cannot, be reconstructed . . . the reconstructed past is not always known with precision."

Having created an at least partially blank space in pre-colonial African society, Malinowski then proceeds with his own form of "backward narration" by first inventing the "pre-European situation [of] absolute sovereignty [of "chiefs"] – complete and undivided power, the right to carry on war and slave raids and to control the wealth of the tribe," (1945:29). Malinowski then fills the African historical void he has created by projecting his prejudices backwards on to pre-colonial African societies (1945:30):

Many African tribes before European contact throve on cannibalism, grew prosperous on slavery or cattle raiding, and developed their political power by intertribal warfare. Would any anthropologist therefore advocate a return to a human flesh diet, or to slavery, or to warfare, and expeditions for loot and booty? Hardly. But does even the fact that his great-grandfathers were accustomed to gorge themselves on human flesh affect in any way, direct or indirect, the desirable diet of a small child in an urban location; or that of a mine laborer; or a member of a tribe who have to devise a new economy because their territory has been cut down, their pastures eroded, and their taxation increased? These questions supply their own answers.

This peculiar juxtaposition of backwards narration with a reference to some of the consequences of colonial exploitation and primitive accumulation seems imaginable only within a functionalist problematic.

CHAPTER ELEVEN

Male African Pastoralists as Failed Capitalists and as "Owners" of Women

Yet another anthropological example of "colonialist criticism" masquerading as social science is readily illustrated by a particular debate on African pastoralist societies. On the one hand, some anthropologists claim that pastoralist social formations are actually capitalist (Schneider 1979) or incipiently capitalist (Paine 1971; Spencer 1984). On the other hand, their "conservatism" prevents them from "taking advantage" of modern, market-oriented economic opportunities. This allows Spencer (1988:23), for example, to assert almost in the same breath that the economy of the Ilmatapato Maasai of Kenya "might usefully be described as one of rudimentary capitalism, just as their pastoralism is essentially a family enterprise"; but, at the same time, "A model of family enterprise and (arguably) of rudimentary capitalism provides the backcloth against which to assess the dynamics of what has proved to be a highly resilient alternative to the market economy."

This opens the way for Spencer (1988:21) to write an ethnography of a Kenya Maasai section which explicitly "has omitted any reference to their involvement in the modern economy." The description of the Meto area [where he did his fieldwork], for instance, "did not elaborate on the Meto 'Center' itself, with its mission station, primary school, shoplets, piped water, and fringe settlement hovering between two cultures. Case 1, which focussed on the response of a family to severe drought, omitted the fact that Masiani's second son, Kunaiju, joined a working party to extend the motor track towards Loodokilani in exchange for some famine relief food and payment from aid agencies" (Spencer 1988:21).

Here, history is deliberately banished from the understanding of a Maasai community in the 1970s and 1980s, which can then be "assessed" according to the universal canons of a naturalized capitalist "human nature," against which the Maasai do not fully measure. There is something *lacking* in their culture and society that prevents them from fully participating in a "modern Kenya." Thus, laments Spencer (1988:23), "There is, I suggest, a more fundamental reason why Maasai generally have not extended *their opportunism* as pastoralists to the market economy in Kenya. This is the importance of time as a utility in a truly capitalist system. Such a concept is quite incompatible with the Maasai conception of time" (emphasis added). Maasai society is "assessed" as deficient in relation to the universal values of "true" capitalism, just as Allen sees "African models" as "pathetically obsessed with racial and cultural confrontation" and "invidious tradition-mongering" and thus incapable of embracing the universal bourgeois "reality."

Pursuing the anthropological analogy with "colonialist criticism" still further, the imposition of Western bourgeois categories on a society grounded in principles and values that are entirely different, if not antithetical, to those of Western society, is seen again in Spencer's discussion of the position of women among Ilmatapato Maasai. The *possibility* that *some* aspects of Maasai social institutions, values, and *Weltanschauungen* may, in fact, be *closer* to a "universal" humanity than those of Western capitalist society does not even cross his mind (Rigby 1992a:166–96).

Spencer continues to base his analysis of Maasai society upon such categorical assertions as these (1988:198): "The undisputed right of *men to own women as possessions* is emphasized by both sexes in Matapato. . . From the outset of their marriage, it is the husband who holds the whip handle, bullying any negligent or defiant wife into submission, rather as he should control a troublesome cow. She is *his possession* and he would lose respect if he overlooks serious lapses" (emphasis added).

The case provided by Spencer in support of these assertions (1988:199–200: Case 41) is one in which a girl disobeys her father's injunctions to continue in an arranged marriage. Ironically, despite being beaten by her reluctant brothers and her father, she wins out eventually, marrying the young man who had been her previous *olmurrani* ("warrior") lover.

Furthermore, at no point does Spencer claim that Maasai use the irregular noun *olopeny* (pl. *iloopeny*) for this male "owner" of women (which would be incorrect), although he does discuss the word in relation to rights in water sources and grazing areas. There is no discussion of its unusual morphology, tonality, or semantics. The only word Maasai use in relation to women is the verb *aitore*, which does not mean "to own," but "to control." The English word "to own" is now so embedded in the capitalist system that it has connotations that could never be attributed to Maasai notions and values (Rigby 1985:166, 142, 146). Presumably, this is another case where Maasai institutions fall short of "universal" (i.e., capitalist) categories of relations between persons and things and among persons.

Yet another example of Spencer's ambiguous (if not contradictory) interpretations of his data is provided by another categorical assertion (1988:39): "There is a prevailing belief that women are *innately dependent on men*. They are held to be constricted in their outlook and abilities, and over all it is they who are responsible for bringing forth life and must be protected together with their children." As with his other propositions, Spencer's own case dealing with women's *responsibilities* (and hence rights) in determining inheritance, succession, and participation in age-set activities and rituals contradicts his own argument. In Case 4 (1988:45), Lolamala's senior wife *determines* the fate of her barren junior co-wife's house (*enkaji*) and its survival as a matricentral unit in the domestic group through the process of transferring by "adoption" her own daughter to the house of this woman. But not only that. When the baby girl dies, the senior wife then arranges for her junior co-wife to adopt one of her own twin sons, thereby making this twin her *step-son*, even when she goes to live with them at the "warrior village" (*emanyata*). Spencer's statement about female weakness and subjugation contains the seeds of its own refutation and dissolution.

But why do lapses like these occur in such an apparently "authoritative" anthropological work, and what are their consequences? The first of these questions can be answered partially by the hoary old notion of the persistence of ethnocentricity, in which English jural concepts are used to translate Maasai terms which mean something else; but they also indicate androcentricity, as well as an ahistorical and uncritical epistemology on the part of the anthropologist, who assumes the universality of Western categories. We are not told anywhere by Spencer how Maasai themselves express this "prevailing belief," for there is no discussion of Maasai concepts of "belief" (*enkirukoto*, from the verb *airuk*, "to believe" or "to have faith"), and how it differs from "knowledge" (*eyiolounoto*, from the verb *ayiolo*, "to know"). Yet we are told that Maasai "speak for themselves" in Spencer's book?

But perhaps the most disturbing misrepresentation of Maasai knowledge and belief is Spencer's use of the term "innately." This is a totally Western concept, linked closely to the spurious arguments invented by bourgeois intellectuals in pursuit of the Holy Grail of genetic, racial, and sexual determinations of cultural and "behavioral" patterns, and could not be further from the thinking and epistemological foundations of Maasai forms of knowledge (Rigby 1991a, 1992a).

Finally, there is no discussion in Spencer's book of how these concepts may have changed over time, particularly as the result of the incorporation of Maasai into the political economy of capitalist colonialism and its post-colonial aftermath. The historical dimensions of these institutions and concepts are entirely ignored, and hence his discussion of gender issues is seriously flawed. A Maasai woman anthropologist, who has focused her research upon changing gender relations, particularly among Kenya Maasai, has clearly stated (Kipuri 1989:121–2):

> From our observation of male–female interactions, we perceive gender parallelism in age-based social formations; and for this reason, we contend that the subjugation of women in such societies is not inherent in the age-set ideology. Rather, it is fundamentally bound up with the circumstances within which these societies have found themselves, especially since their integration within pre-capitalist, colonial, and post-colonial states.

If *any* generalizations can be made, then, about the concepts of ownership, property, and possession in Maasai and similar social formations, they must be made upon some such lines as the following (Kipuri 1989:120–1; cf. Rigby 1985, 1992a):

> [We] . . . conclude that, although women's rights to the means of production were quite extensive, they were limited in the same way men's were. This makes it difficult to devalue women's rights on this account or to support the claim that men have absolute rights over

them. Rather than make the point that women may also "own" the means of production . . . it would be more accurate to emphasize that in most age-based societies, no one really "owned" anything; instead, rights were at best limited to use-rights. This is because "ownership" as we know it in western capitalist contexts carries very different connotations in most age-based societies; indeed, to most of them, the concept will be foreign.

And Kipuri adds, for good measure (1989:117), that in Maasai society, "women cannot be seen to constitute an exploited class, unless we see them as exploiting themselves for the benefit of their sons."

Apart from the colonialist epistemology underlying Spencer's misrepresentations of Maasai institutions, the practical consequences of, for example, gender relations as propounded by him are immense. As the role of women becomes a dominant issue in planning development strategies and priorities for Maasai and other pastoral peoples, the idea that women's subjugation among them is primarily as the result of features intrinsic to their social formations, rather than as products of colonialist and capitalist incorporation and commoditization, can have serious and deleterious effects on their future. Instead of *exposing* the hidden exploitation and social disruption created by untoward historical circumstances, which should be the true subjects of an authentic and historically conscious anthropology, the anthropologist here is merely aiding and abetting the mythologizing of the Maasai which has been so characteristic of colonialist and racist conceptions of them, constituting a real danger to them (Knowles and Collett 1989).

Certain forms of contemporary anthropological work and discourse, far from subverting the misrepresentation of Africa and African societies, contribute to the myths about, and distortions of, African cultures in literature as in the popular media. As such, anthropology appears as just another form of "colonialist discourse/criticism," failing utterly in its aims and responsibilities (McGrane 1989).

But furthermore, let me reiterate that the burden of this book has also been to demonstrate a direct analogy between distortions in anthropological knowledge on the one hand, and the massive assault upon peoples of African descent in the Western world by well-funded racist "research" being conducted by particular groups of white, Western, predominantly male intellectuals on the other. Only alienated forms of analytical thought can produce perverse knowledges of this kind.

PART THREE

Theoretical Coda

Marxism is a nineteenth-century paradigm which presented itself as a natural science of society that not only had an intellectual identity but also a political one. It was a grand theory to be enacted and measured against history. In the period of Parsonian hegemony in the United States, Marxism maintained itself as an alternative, suppressed and awaiting its release. Today, there are still those who desire to preserve the framework, dogma, and canonic terminology – formalists like Maurice Godelier and Louis Althusser. But there are also more interpretive Marxists, accepting the framework loosely as a realm of shared discourse, but probing within it to find out in cultural and experiential terms what concepts such as modes of production, commodity fetishism, and relations and forces of production might mean under diverse and changing world conditions ... There is indeed a new empirical, and essentially ethnographic/documentary mood in Marxist writing (see Anderson 1984)... While Marxism as a system of thought remains strong as an image, in practice, it is difficult to identify Marxists anymore, or to locate a contemporary central tradition for it (Marcus and Fischer 1986:11–12).

In an age of the need to de-center and globalize social theory, especially in anthropology, which is supposed to be **aware** of what and how people are thinking in the places where anthropological research is still predominantly carried out (the "Third World"), the white Euro-American-centricity of such statements is astounding; and reference to Perry Anderson's book, which is explicitly focused upon developments in European Marxism, merely compounds the crime (cf. Amin 1989).

It is here that interpretative anthropology loses entirely its claim to "critical theory" (Fay 1987), and moves into the field of incestuous literary criticism. The subject becomes the "anthropologist as author" (Geertz 1988) and the objects of anthropological

discourse cease to be real peoples, the production and reproduction of their social life and communities, their exploitation and
suffering, and their attempts to fight back: they become the
producers of texts, which it is the anthropologist's job to
"interpret." Knowledge and the ontology of "facts" becomes the
privileged domain of expert discourse, totally divorced from the
social, intellectual, and discursive space occupied by real people;
it becomes the property of those who would wield power. As a
result, social facts no longer need to attain or demonstrate
authenticity; their authority derives from their status as an
emanation of assumed intellectual, and actual political, power.

CHAPTER TWELVE

Marxism and Anthropology I: "Objectivity," Relativism, and the World Economic System

If Durkheim and the Durkheimians temporarily won their Pyrrhic victory over their insistence upon the separation of theory and political and intellectual *praxis* in the social sciences in general and anthropology in particular, Marxist anthropology has often fallen foul of, or at least demonstrated a curious lethargy towards, the chasm which exists between the theoretically sophisticated manipulation of anthropological data on the one hand, and the theoretical status of the production of these ethnographic data on the other (Rigby 1985:25–47). This has serious consequences for the claim of Marxist anthropology to speak "for the people" in their struggle against domination and exploitation, and for revolutionary *praxis*. Fabian's statement reinforces this position (1983:155):

> The question of Marxist anthropology is not resolved in my mind. In part this is so because we have ... as yet little Marxist praxis at the level of the production of ethnographic knowledge. As long as such a practical basis is lacking or badly developed, most of what goes by the name of Marxist anthropology amounts to little more than theoretical exercises in the style of Marx and Engels. These exercises have their merits: the best among them have helped to confound earlier approaches and analyses. They are bound to remain disconnected forays, however, as long as their authors share with bourgeois positivist anthropology certain fundamental assumptions concerning the nature of ethnographic data and the use of "objective" methods.

A brief survey of selected fieldwork studies by Marxist anthropologists reveals either little interest in this question, or relatively unquestioned acceptance of "standard" anthropological fieldwork methods and assumptions characteristic of non-Marxist anthropology. Godelier, for example, in his study *The Making of Great Men* among the Baruya of New Guinea (1986 [1982]) is overtly concerned primarily with the ethics of fieldwork and the need not to divulge "secret" ethnographic information. While he explains admirably his focus upon male domination and its supporting ideology in Baruya society with reference to the failure of a naïve class analysis to explain racism and sexism, he asserts a form of relativism as his major comment on the theory of fieldwork (Godelier 1986:viii):

> One may easily imagine, on reading these pages, just how much time and confidence it must have taken on the part of the Baruya to introduce me to their way of thinking and allow me to see (as they expressed it) not only the leaves, branches, and the trunk, but also some of the most secretly buried roots of their thought. I must ask the reader who may sometimes be tempted, according to the lights of his or her own philosophy or mood, to regard the secrets confided in me by the Baruya as derisory, grotesque, or even obscene, to remember that for them they are an essential part of their identity, a vital, sacred force, inherited from the past, on which they depend in order to withstand all those voluntary or involuntary pressures that our world brings to bear upon them, often enough in perfectly good faith but more often still deliberately. An anthropologist cannot side with those who, deliberately or unaware, despite [*sic*] and/or destroy the society they wish to know and make known. Knowledge is not a game without consequences. Every society has its secrets that it protects and protect it. To hand them carelessly over to the public without debate or precaution would not merely be treacherous but irresponsible, but would actually pervert the work of scientific investigation into a force of aggression or domination.

There is moral rectitude here, but no reflexivity. And while relativism has played an important role in "de-ethno-centering" anthropology, we must remember that its intellectual pedigree goes back to Comte's positivism and its inescapable "reverence for established authority" (Marcuse 1955:355), the very obverse of Marxist praxis and theory. Durkheim's debt to Comte in his conception of a positivist science of society is clear; to this must be added the inheritance of a necessary dominance of relativism in structural–functional anthropology through both Radcliffe-Brown and Malinowski and their students. This inheritance, in turn, brings down to us all the other baggage it entails. As Marcuse notes (1955:353, 354, 357):

> According to Comte, relativism is inseparable from the conception that sociology is an exact science dealing with invariant laws of social statics and dynamics . . . The process of making social theory compatible with existing conditions is not complete . . . [until] . . . elements that would transcend or point beyond the validity of the given matters . . . [are] . . . excluded; this requires that social theory be made relativistic. The last decisive aspect of positivism . . . Science, to Comte, is the field of theoretical relativism, and the latter the area from which "value judgements" are excluded . . . The positivist program for social reform foreshadows liberalism's turn into authoritarianism.

I wonder what happened to Marx among the Baruya?

Furthermore, although Godelier does provide a brief sketch of Baruya history in relation to neighboring peoples and language groups (1986:1–4), this history does not really inform the succeeding analysis except, perhaps, in his penultimate chapter on "recent transformations in Baruya society," dealing with the colonial period.

For Maurice Bloch, on the other hand, history becomes a crucial epistemological tool for the understanding of circumcision rituals among the Merina of Madagascar. This awareness of the imperatives of history influences the whole process of his study, from fieldwork to fruition (Bloch 1986: ix):

> This book has been almost fifteen years in the making because, when I started to produce a study that combined anthropological research and primary historical research, I did not realize the sheer practical difficulties of the enterprise. It is an attempt to combine knowledge of the intimate interconnections of all aspects of life and the subjective empathy, which are the main values of participant observation, with the historical perspective, which is necessary to face up genuinely to the sociological questions and wider theoretical issues the material presents.

So, too, for Donham, history becomes basic to any understanding of the Maale social formation of south-western Ethiopia

(1985, 1990). But since Donham's analysis is a Marxist one, not any old history will do. A critical history of social formations in the entire region in which the Maale are situated becomes not only a pre-condition to understanding Maale social organization, it also constitutes an essential component of Donham's epistemological framework. As with Bloch, it also directs (however vaguely at first) his fieldwork (Donham 1985:1):

> I want to recount how two very different images of the Maale . . . guided my research (often in only half-conscious ways) and how I came to see one as considerably more useful than the other . . . The first image is one of a traditional African kingdom which has somehow survived into the present, an isolated society, uninfluenced by social forces like western colonial governments, cash cropping, or migrant labor that long ago transformed the lives of other peoples. This image calls up notions of well-integrated, "primitive" communities of kinsmen and of divine kings who magically insure the fertility of crops and people. The second image, in contrast, is a great deal less exotic and, at first glance, perhaps less arresting: this is the idea of a peasantry, neither isolated nor self-contained, but a constituent part of a larger, stratified social system. Located towards the lower economic and political rungs, most peasants today play a role in the world economic system. One immediately thinks of hard work, factionalism, and domination by "outsiders."

Donham then provides both a sophisticated materialist problematic appropriate to his task of understanding the Maale social formation in the present, and a detailed historical exposition of how the second "image" was the only one that could represent authentically the Maale experience.

Yet there is little consideration in any of these studies of how the ethnographic data so brilliantly elaborated were produced. And it seems that we find a concern with this fundamental problem primarily among anthropologists whose work is informed by linguistic theory, sometimes accompanied by elements of historical materialism.

CHAPTER THIRTEEN

Marxism and Anthropology II: Fieldwork and Language in History and the Context of Knowledge Production

Friedrich, in his book *The Princes of Naranja*, significantly sub-titled *An Essay in Anthropological Method*, is intensely concerned with how knowledge is produced in the fieldwork context, and how this is transformed into an ethnographic text. At the explicitly recognized risk of eclecticism ("even before fieldwork my eclectic background made me feel that the general anthropology of the time with its five fields of language, culture, human biology, prehistory, and personality, was too narrow for me"), Friedrich cheerfully recognizes the influence upon his work of relativism, romanticism, structural–functionalism, rationalism, Marxism, Freudianism, and phenomenology (1986a:258–9).

Although Friedrich begins his fieldwork in Mexico in Spanish, he later realizes the need to use Tarascan (1986a:206). His linguistic interests then allow him to penetrate the crucial importance of political ideology in the "self-awareness" of the community of Naranja, an awareness linked to its earlier "agrarian revolt" (Friedrich 1970). Then he notes (1986a:241):

> Political ideology was clearly overdeveloped in Naranja to the point of becoming a cultural hypertrophy; many leaders are clear about factional structures, the role of Communism in the state, techniques for gaining power, and so forth, and often discourse about them in a sophisticated way. But Naranja is not all that different from many other communities with a developed or even exacerbated (self-)awareness, often the result of specific, historical causes.

In *The Princes of Naranja*, Friedrich stops short of developing a
Marxist theory of language; this is, in part, due to his still somewhat
undigested eclecticism. But his concern with "ideology" leads him
to a more extended discourse on language (published in the same
year), in which he deals (if only in passing) with the potentiality of
Marxist theory for illuminating critical areas of linguistic
understanding. Thus he notes (1986b:44):

> As Marx and others have argued, even the most completely elaborated
> ideological representations find their way into language . . . As these
> ideological representations find their way into language they become
> subject, not only to habitual classification and grammatical processing
> . . . but to analogical transformations of all kinds, ambiguity and
> marking, the play of tropes, polarization, condensation, and so forth.
> Thus, as propounded by Lefebvre, "A sociology inspired by Marxism
> might well address itself to the relation between . . . poetry and myth"
> (1977:261).

Friedrich, for reasons that should now be obvious, finds it
necessary to add a caveat: "Here, however, I would insist on the
inadequacies of any sociological or heavily sociocentric approach,
because the poetic use of language is so largely a matter, not only
of society, but of the unique imagination." I need only add that a
Marxist phenomenology would seek to go beyond the simple
dichotomy between "society" and "the unique imagination"; and
Friedrich himself almost admits as much (1986b:98):

> In symbolic studies today a major theoretical enterprise or exploration
> is to be explicit about subjective factors and to explicitly relate one's
> authorial subjectivity to what used to be called objective analysis. These
> explorations, depending on the author, may derive from a new-Marxian
> epistemology or an Orientalist, existentialist, or phenomenological
> philosophy or (in my case) as analogy from the principle of
> indeterminacy in physics ("the observer is an integral part of the
> universe of observation"). Whatever the sources – and they must be
> multiple in all cases – I subscribe to these explorations.

This discussion of Friedrich's work may have taken us far from
Africa; yet it brings us back to critical anthropologists such as
Johannes Fabian. His interests in the crucial dimension of language
in history and anthropological fieldwork in Zaire (1986:2,5; 1990)
leads him to a trenchant critique of the reduction of language in

fieldwork to a mere "tool, vehicle, or receptacle" for the "collection of data" (1983:106–9), or to what Radcliffe-Brown called "their acts of speech" (1952:190). The production of social knowledge can be authentic only if it is based upon a common discourse of subjects and coevality in time, place,and power (Fabian 1983; Rigby 1985, 1992a, 1994).

There are thus at least three levels upon which the praxis of Marxist anthropology must be manifest: first, the "objective" contextualization of the societies or communities in which anthropologists study, in their historical specificities of regional and global political economy as a necessary condition for their understanding; second, the practice of fieldwork based upon a critical theory of the production of social knowledge; and third, the political praxis which combines the first two with heightened awareness and political mobilization. This entails a radical critique of cultural imperialism, leading to an anti-hegemonic struggle.

The first level is evident in much contemporary Marxist anthropology; the second is more explicit in works by linguistically trained anthropologists, or bourgeois problematics such as those of post-modernist discourse or interpretative anthropology. If Marxist anthropology is truly to represent the historical and cultural experience of a social formation by producing a knowledge which is at least partially congruent with the politico-economic and discursive space occupied by the subjects themselves, then a historical materialist theory of language and a phenomenology of the *context* of knowledge production in the field must be devised; they are "two sides of the same coin." But the epistemology of neither can be assumed; they must be rigorously theorized (cf. Mudimbe 1991; Rigby 1991a). Only then can anthropological knowledge become accessible to the third level, that of political praxis. This book is offered as a small contribution towards the achievement of that end.

Appendix

The U.S. Invasion of Somalia; Rwanda and the Western Media

Contained in this Appendix are three letters, one on the United States invasion of Somalia and two on the misrepresentations of the crisis in Rwanda by the Western mainstream press. They were sent to *The Philadelphia Inquirer* (*PI*) and/or the *New York Times* (*NYT*) on the dates indicated. None of them were published in those "journals of record." A version of the Somali letter, however, was published in the *New Vision* newspaper in Kampala, Uganda, in August 1993, and received a generally favorable response from my Ugandan compatriots.

Somalia, the U.S., and The Forgetting of History

[7 October 1993: sent to both *PI* and *NYT*]

In the context of the current Western hysteria about what is happening in Somalia, we need to be reminded of a number of issues that have been lost; or, perhaps, they have been conveniently and deliberately forgotten? The latter is more likely, because their absence from press reports and the public pronouncements of politicians allows a number of myths about U.S. military intervention in Somalia to survive and yet others to be instantly created.

The first is the fabrication that the state of contemporary Somali society can be understood apart from the history of the "Horn of Africa" as a whole, including Ethiopia, Eritrea and Djibouti, as well as that of Kenya, Sudan, and Uganda. Since Somali independence in 1960, it has been the object of super-power manipulations. During the first half of Mohammed Siad Barre's dictatorship, established by a coup in 1969, Soviet influence grew steadily. As a result of events in neighboring Ethiopia and Kenya, however, Siad Barre switched his allegiance to the

U.S. during the last 12 years of his regime.

It was Siad Barre who destroyed the independent Somali state, reducing the basis of his power to the loyalty of three clans: his own (Marehan), his mother's (Ogaden), and his son-in-law's (Dulbahante), provoking Somalis to label his regime a "Family" called "the MOD."

The second popular canard is the product of the myth-makers in Washington DC and their powerful patrons representing U.S. business interests. As early as 1980, congressman Solarz was counseling the Carter Administration to stay out of Somalia because it had neither strategic nor economic significance for the United States (*New York Times*, 6 July 1980). This was pure pretense, in blatant contradiction to authoritative contemporary reports, put out at a time the U.S. was already planning support for Barre's Somalia, and as a direct result of growing Soviet weight in Ethiopia after the 1974 overthrow of Haile Selassie and the débâcle of the Ogaden was of the mid-1970s.

By 1978, with Cuban help, Ethiopia had re-occupied the major part of the Ogaden, and Somalia was again ripe for Western manipulation, with Siad Barre waiting with open arms. Throughout these struggles, and up to the present, scant attention was given by the super-power strategists to the sufferings of the African peoples of the Horn, particularly the Somalis. In fact, the mainstream Western press as well has exhibited nothing but contempt for the Somalian people since their current operation began. This has led to further Western inventions about Somalis and their society.

In the early stages the U.S. public were told that all Somalis were stoned out of their minds every day when, in fact, they chew a very mild stimulant no stronger than caffeine. More recently, when they have shown considerable military skill and success, the Somali people have been labelled "barbaric" and accused of "atrocities" by Major David Stockwell, chief UNOSOM (read U.S.) spokesman, and others (*New York Times*, 6 October, 1993). United States and other UN forces have bombarded and destroyed Somali homes and buildings in Mogadishu, killing women and children in their misguided attempts to demonize and blame Gen. Mohamed Farrah Aidid as a "warlord" responsible for all aggression in the capital; but these are not atrocities!

It is hardly surprising, then, that the ostensible humanitarian motives of current U.S. policy in Somalia are seriously compromised by the little publicized (covered up?) role of United States oil companies in the design and implementation of that policy. In the final years before the overthrow of Somalia's (by then pro-United States) dictator, Mohammed Siad Barre, oil development rights to nearly two-thirds of the entire area of the country were allocated to the American oil giants Conoco, Amoco, Chevron, and Phillips. Conoco maintained an office in Mogadishu throughout the period of Somalia's current crisis, from 1991 until U.S.

intervention in 1993 (*Philadelphia Inquirer*, 19 January, 1993). We are told that these companies are "sitting on a prospective fortune in exclusive concessions to explore and exploit tens of millions of acres of the Somalian countryside." And we also know that Mohamed Farrah Aidid knows all about it. Quite simply, he knows too much; and it doesn't take a genius to put two and two together.

It is also widely known that while the U.S. and some other U.N. contingents in Somalia (notably the Belgians in Kismayu) are waging war upon the Somalian people, yet others are still attempting to pursue the U.N.'s original and purportedly humanitarian mandate in that sad country. For example, the military contingent from Botswana who were based in Bardera, were reported by the BBC in August to be able to wander the streets often unarmed, to co-operate with the relief organizations, and to make friends with the Somali people without firing a shot. During concurrent periods of violence and slaughter in Mogadishu and Kismayu, only one Somali had been killed in Bardera.

Do the movers and shakers and the powers-that-be think they can keep everyone ignorant of the truth all of the time?

Rwanda, Africa, and The Western Press

[9 May 1994: sent to *PI*]

At last there is a glimmer of hope that the Western media have taken one small step in the direction of understanding something about what is happening in Rwanda. Keith Richburg's report in *The Inquirer* of May 9th, 1994, takes that tiny step by showing that the conflict is the result of a "systematic campaign of killing directed by political leaders and backed by the military." It is in the interests of unscrupulous politicians that it is interpreted instead as a spontaneous "tribal" explosion.

But even in this relatively enlightened report, the tell-tale signs of Western misconceptions about Africa and Africans show through. The Tutsi and Hutu are still called "tribes" throughout the piece; and, in a previous dispatch, Terry Leonard of the Associated Press conjures up Rwandan "savagery" (*Inquirer* 5/8/94), an epithet never applied to Bosnia or slaughter in western societies. The Rwandan embroilment is, in fact, thoroughly modern, and is about land, wealth, and political power in a weak post-colonial state.

No amount of explanation can diminish the horror of Rwanda; but then again, is it of any help in Bosnia? Given the continued misrepresentation of the Rwandan case, however, some effort must be made to set the record straight.

As with other African conflicts, the civil war in Rwanda is regularly attributed by the Western media to primordial "tribal" identities and hostility; murder and mayhem in Bosnia and the rest of the world are classified as "ethnic" or "religious." It is significant that the one first-hand account by a Munyarwanda (a citizen of Rwanda) published earlier by you makes no reference to "tribe," and only once uses the term "ethnic Tutsi." The media instances of the "tribal" misnomer are too numerous to list.

Prior to nineteenth-century colonial occupation, first by the Germans and then by Belgium after 1916 (mandated by the League of Nations in 1919), Rwanda, like its neighbor Burundi, was a class-stratified monarchic state with three major classes. The Batutsi (singular, Mututsi), an aristocratic ruling class, were primarily cattle-keepers from amongst whom the royal lineage (the Abanyinginya) and the King (Mwami) derived. They made up about 19% of the population. The largest class, the Bahutu (singular, Muhutu), were predominantly agriculturalist "commoners" who constituted about 80% of the Rwandan people. A tiny group of gatherer-hunters, the Batwa, made up the final less than one percent.

Many Bahutu, however, owned cattle and other livestock, while many Batutsi were relatively impoverished agriculturalists: the major classes were thus internally differentiated by status and rank. Both classes shared a common language, overall cultural institutions, and clan names, and they intermarried. This complex of class, descent, status, and power has been variously described by outsiders as a "feudal," "caste," or "tributary" system. Whatever the nomenclature, all reliable historical evidence indicates a relation of *interdependence* within the system of relatively mild domination, a relation called *ubuhake* by the Rwandan people.

All this was dismantled by colonialism, leading to a vastly transformed, fragmented political system by the time of independence from Belgian colonial control. Even the institutions of lineage and kinship solidarity shared by both classes were seriously weakened. The colonial system of "indirect rule," invented elsewhere in Africa by the British but practiced by the Belgians, converted some Batutsi into colonial petty dictators over the rest of the people, Batutsi and Bahutu alike. The essentially authoritarian and exploitative structures of imperialist hegemony, exacerbated by huge and growing differentials in wealth and power, were what the Banyarwanda inherited from the Belgians.

Although "traditional" identity labels ("Tutsi," "Hutu") are used as ideological categories in the present conflict, this is class war in its most heightened and poignant form and is of recent historical provenance. To make matters worse, the Western powers refer their proposed actions to the Belgians for approval, thus consulting the country most despised in Rwanda for its previous exploitation of the country, a far from benign memory for most Rwandans, Tutsi or Hutu.

What is happening in Rwanda, then, is a contemporary war conducted

under the conditions of neo-colonial hegemony; it has nothing to do with
"tribes" from a mythical, primordial, "savage" past.

Rwanda and the Western Media: Malice Toward Whom?

[23 August 1994: sent to *PI*]

As the true history and basis of the present crisis in Rwanda become more
evident to the mainstream Western media, there has been a
corresponding, if slight, improvement in coverage of the tragedy. Earlier
uncritical (and erroneous) characterizations of the conflict as being a
spontaneous "tribal war," involving two distinct "tribes," the Hutu and
the Tutsi, and dating from the remote, pre-colonial past of east-central
Africa, have given way to more sober descriptions of "predominantly"
Hutu and/or Tutsi groupings, and "Tutsi- and Hutu-led" movements.

Yet the gross misrepresentations of African politics in general and
recent Rwandan history in particular as being entirely caused by
"tribalism" are fostered by editorial-page pieces such as Jonathan Power's
("Tribalism Lives in Africa"), published in *The Inquirer* on July 30, and
television reports like that by Barry Peterson on CBS, broadcast on July
31 last, when he called the Rwandan struggle "tribal warfare that has been
going on for 800 years." Both pieces were rubbish. What is happening in
Rwanda is a contemporary, thoroughly modern class conflict over land,
wealth, and power; it has nothing to do with "tribes" left over from a
mythical, primordial, "savage," past.

It was with great disappointment, then, that I read your brief editorial,
"Malice Toward None," in *The Inquirer* of August 22. Although your
intentions are estimable, the thrust of your comments is to put the Rwanda
Patriotic Front (RPF) on the defensive. This implication flies in the face
of the real situation.

1. You state that the "new Rwandan government *claims* to be seeking
    reconciliation": it *is* actively doing so.
2. You charge the "new government" with convincing Hutu refugees that
    they may return safely to their country. The RPF government has
    strenuously tried to do so. But you omit the crucial fact that members
    of the deposed Rwandan government and armed forces of the late
    President Habyarimana are waging a war of physial intimidation and
    propaganda in the Rwandan refugee camps in Zaire, claiming non-
    existent massacres of Bahutu by the "Tutsi-led" RPF. This is a
    continuation of the systematic campaign of killing and mystification,
    the *real* massacres, directed by the political leaders of the previous
    government before it was overthrown, backed by the army. It is in

the interests of unscrupulous politicians that the conflict be interpreted as a spontaneous tribal explosion.

3. You urge the Kigali government to "expand confidence-building measures, such as sharing power with the Hutu majority." You do not point out that, according to your own sources, both the President (Bizimungu) and the Prime Minister (Twagiramungu) under the RPF government are Bahutu, and that the leadership *and* the rank and file of both its civilian and military wings include Batutsi and Bahutu. Furthermore, the head of the Hutu-dominated *Interahamwe*, the group responsible for the slaughter of thousands of Batutsi, is from the Tutsi class!

4. The RPF has already invited international human rights monitoring of the reconciliation and re-building process and the prosecution of those responsible for the massacres. They don't need any coaxing by the West and its press to do so.

5. The only positive point in your editorial is the final one: that humanitarian aid should be given primarily to Rwandans returning home, a conclusion entirely in agreement with stated RPF policies and positions.

Why, then, we may ask, the negative gravamen of your editorial toward the new RPF government, which has been praised by numerous international agencies and organizations for its principled approach to Rwanda's rehabilitation? The only answer I can think of is that the Western press cannot credit *any* African organization with the integrity, ability, and responsibility to solve contemporary African problems. This smacks of a patronizing, nineteenth-century racism. *I* know for a fact that the National Resistance Movement in my own country, Uganda, under our President Yoweri Museveni, has achieved a near miracle of reconciliation and transformation in the eight years it has had the responsibility for government, after a protracted war of liberation against our previous Ugandan oppressors. The RPF is quite capable of achieving the same for Rwanda.

Bibliography

Achebe, Chinua. 1989. *Hopes and Impediments*. New York: Doubleday.

Allen, Philip A. 1971. "*Bound to Violence* by Yambo Ouologuem," *Pan African Journal*, 4:518-23.

Allen, Robert. 1990. *Black Awakening in Capitalist America*. Trenton, New Jersey: Africa World Press.

Amin, Samir. 1980. *Class and Nation, Historically and in The Current Crisis*. New York: Monthly Review.

——. 1989. *Eurocentrism*, translated by Russell Moore. New York: Monthly Review.

——. 1992. *Empire of Chaos*. New York: Monthly Review.

Amselle, Jean-Loupe and Elikia M'Bokolo (eds). 1985. *Au coeur de l'ethnie: Ethnies, tribalisme et Etat en Afrique*. Paris: Editions La Découverte.

Anderson, Perry. 1984. *In the Tracks of Historical Materialism*. Chicago: University of Chicago Press.

Appiah, Kwame A. 1992. *In My Father's House: Africa in the Philosophy of Culture*. New York: Oxford University Press.

——. 1993. "Europe Upside Down: The Fallacies of the New Afrocentrism," *SAPINA Bulletin*, 5:1-8.

Asad, Talal. 1973. "Introduction" in Talal Asad (ed.): *Anthropology and the Colonial Encounter*. Atlantic Highlands, New Jersey: Humanities Press.

——. 1993. *Genealogies of Religion: Discipline and Reasons of Power in Christianity and Islam*. Baltimore, Maryland: The Johns Hopkins University Press.

Augé, Marc. 1982. *The Anthropological Circle: Symbol, Function, History*, translated by Martin Thorn. Cambridge: Cambridge University Press.

Azoulay, Katya Gibel. 1994. "Appropriating Anthropology: The Space for Race," *SAPINA Bulletin*, 6:13-29.

Baker, John R. 1974. *Race*. London: Oxford University Press.

Baker, Lee D. 1994a. "The Role of Anthropology in the Social Construction of Race, 1896-1954." Philadelphia: Ph.D. Dissertation, Department of Anthropology, Temple University.

——. 1994b. "The Location of Franz Boas Within the African-American Struggle," *Critique of Anthropology*, 14:199–217.

Barnett, Tony and Piers Blaikie. 1992. *Aids in Africa: Its Present and Future Impact*. New York: The Guilford Press.

Barrett, Stanley R. 1984. *The Rebirth of Anthropological Theory*. Toronto: University of Toronto Press.

Bates, Robert H., Valentin Y. Mudimbe, and Jean O'Barr (eds). 1993. *Africa and the Disciplines: Contributions of Research in Africa to the Social Sciences and Humanities*. Chicago: The University of Chicago Press.

Bell, Derrick. 1987. *And We Are Not Saved*. New York: Basic Books.

Blakey, Michael L. 1987. "Skull Doctors: Intrinsic Social and Political Bias in the History of American Physical Anthropology," *Critique of Anthropology*, 7:7–35.

——. 1991. "Man and Nature, White and Other," in Faye V. Harrison (ed.). *Decolonizing Anthropology: Moving Further Toward an Anthropology for Liberation*. Washington, D.C.: Association of Black Anthropologists/ American Anthropological Association.

Bloch, Maurice. 1986. *From Blessing to Violence: History and Ideology in the Circumcision Ritual of the Merina of Madagascar*. Cambridge: Cambridge University Press.

Bohannan, Paul. 1960a. "Patterns of Murder and Suicide," in Paul Bohannan (ed.). *African Homicide and Suicide*. Princeton, New Jersey: Princeton University Press.

——. (ed.). 1960b. *African Homicide and Suicide*. Princeton, New Jersey: Princeton University Press.

Bovin, Mette. 1972. "Ethno-Terms for Ethnic Groups: Examples From Azande and Kanuri," in André Singer and Brian V. Street (eds): *Zande Themes*. Oxford: Basil Blackwell.

Brantlinger, Patrick. 1988. *Rule of Darkness: British Literature and Imperialism, 1830–1914*. Ithaca, New York: Cornell University Press.

——. 1990. *Crusoe's Footprints: Cultural Studies in Britain and America*. New York: Routledge.

Burkhalter, S. Brian. 1991. "If Only They Would Listen: The Anthropology of Business and the Business of Anthropology," in Aaron Podolefski and Peter J. Brown (eds): *Applying Cultural Anthropology*. Mountain View, California: Mayfield Publishing Company.

Burton, Richard. 1967 [1876]. *Two Trips to Gorilla Land and the Cataracts of the Congo*. New York: Johnson.

Cain, D.P. and C.H. Vanderwolf. 1990. "A Critique of Rushton on Race, Brain Size and Intelligence," *Personality and Individual Differences*, 11:777–84.

Cashmore, Ellis. 1984. "Ethnicity," in *Dictionary of Race and Ethnic Relations*. London: Routledge.

Catalano, Joseph S. 1986. *A Commentary on Jean-Paul Sartre's "Critique of*

Dialectical Reason", Volume 1. Chicago: University of Chicago Press.

Césaire, Aimé. 1972 [1955]. *Discourse on Colonialism,* translated by Joan Pinkham. New York: Monthly Review.

Cheru, Fantu. 1989. *The Silent Revolution in Africa: Debt, Development and Democracy.* London: Zed Books Limited.

Chirimuuta, Richard and Rosalind. 1989 [1987]. *Aids, Africa and Racism.* London: Free Association Books.

Clifford, James. 1988. *The Predicament of Culture: Twentieth Century Ethnography, Literature, and Art.* Cambridge, Massachusetts: Harvard University Press.

Clifford, James and George E. Marcus (eds). 1986. *Writing Culture: The Poetics and Politics of Ethnography.* Berkeley, California: University of California Press.

Cohen, Mitchell. 1993. "Somalia: the Cynical Manipulation of Hunger," *Z Magazine,* 6:33–6.

Cohen, William B. 1980. *The French Encounter With Africans.* Bloomington, Indiana: Indiana University Press.

Comaroff, Jean and John. 1991. *Of Revelation and Revolution: Christianity, Colonialism, and Consciousness in South Africa.* Chicago: University of Chicago Press.

Conrad, Joseph. 1950 [1899]. *Heart of Darkness.* New York: New American Library.

Cook, P.J. and G.H. Zarkin. 1985. "Crime and the Business Cycle," *Journal of Legal Studies,* 14:115–28.

Cox, Oliver C. 1948. *Caste, Class, and Race: a Study in Social Dynamics.* New York: Doubleday and Co. Inc.

Davidson, Basil. 1992. *The Black Man's Burden: Africa and the Curse of the Nation-State.* New York: Times Books.

Davis, David Brion. 1966. *The Problem of Slavery in Western Culture.* Ithaca, New York: Cornell University Press.

——. 1984. *Slavery and Human Progress.* New York: Oxford University Press.

Diamond, Stanley. 1974. *In Search of the Primitive.* New Brunswick, New Jersey: Transaction Books.

Diop, Cheikh Anta. 1974 [1955]. *The African Origin of Civilization: Myth or Reality,* translated by Mercer Cook. Westport, Connecticut: Lawrence Hill.

Donham, Donald. 1985. *Work and Power in Maale, Ethiopia.* Ann Arbor, Michigan: UMI Research Press.

——. 1990. *History, Power, Ideology: Central Issues in Marxism and Anthropology.* Cambridge/Paris: Cambridge University Press/Éditions de la Maison des Sciences de l'Homme.

Du Bois, W.E.B. 1962 [1932]. *Black Reconstruction in America, 1869–1880.* Cleveland, Ohio: Meridian.

——. 1981 [1946]. *The World and Africa: An Inquiry Into the Part Which Africa has Played in World History.* New York: International Publishers.

Du Couret, Louis. 1854. *Voyages au pays des Niam-Niams ou hommes a queue.* Paris: Calmann Lévy.

Ehret, Christopher. 1971. *Southern Nilotic History: Linguistic Approaches to the Study of the Past.* Evanston, Illinois: Northwestern University Press.

Ellis, Lee. 1990. "Universal Behavioral and Demographic Correlations of Criminal Behavior: Toward Common Ground in the Assessment of Criminological Theories," in Lee Ellis and Harry Hoffman (eds): *Crime in Biological, Social, and Moral Contexts.* New York: Praeger.

Ellis, Lee and Harry Hoffman (eds). 1990. *Crime in Biological, Social, and Moral Contexts.* New York: Praeger.

Ensminger, Jean. 1992. *Making a Market: The Institutional Transformation of an African Society.* Cambridge: Cambridge University Press.

Evans-Pritchard, E.E. 1937. *Witchcraft, Oracles, and Magic Among the Azande.* Oxford: The Clarendon Press.

——. 1958. "The Ethnic Composition of the Azande of Central Africa," *Anthropological Quarterly,* 31:95–118.

——. 1981. *A History of Anthropological Thought.* London: Faber and Faber.

Fabian, Johannes. 1983. *Time and the Other: How Anthropology Makes its Object.* New York: Columbia University Press.

——. 1986. *Language and Colonial Power: The Appropriation of Swahili in the Former Belgian Congo, 1880–1938.* Cambridge: Cambridge University Press.

——. 1990. *Power and Performance: Ethnographic Explorations Through Proverbial Wisdom and Theater.* Madison, Wisconsin: University of Wisconsin Press.

Fanon, Frantz. 1965 [1961]. *The Wretched of the Earth,* translated by Constance Farrington and with a Preface by Jean-Paul Sartre. London: MacGibbon and Key.

——. 1967 [1952]. *Black Skin, White Masks,* translated by Charles L. Markmann. New York: Grove Press.

Farmer, Paul. 1994. *The Uses of Haiti.* Monroe, Maine: Common Courage Press.

Fay, Brian. 1987. *Critical Social Science: Liberation and its Limits.* Ithaca, New York: Cornell University Press.

Fields, Barbara. 1990. "Slavery, Race and Ideology in the United States of America," *New Left Review,* 181:95–118.

Flynn, James R. 1980. *Race, IQ and Jensen.* London: Routledge and Kegan Paul.

Forbes, Patrick E. 1969 [1849]. *Six Months' Service in the African Blockade.* London: Dawsons.

Fox, Richard (ed.). 1991. *Recapturing Anthropology: Working in the Present.* Santa Fe, New Mexico: School of American Research Press.

Fox-Genovese, E. and Eugene Genovese. 1983. *Fruits of Merchant Capital: Slavery and Bourgeois Property in the Rise and Expansion of Capitalism.* Oxford: Oxford University Press.

Franke, Richard W. and Barbara H. Chasin. 1980. *Seeds of Famine: Ecological Destruction and the Development Dilemma in The West African Sahel.* Montclair, New Jersey: Allenheld, Osmun.

Fredrickson, George M. 1971. *The Black Image in the White Mind: The Debate on Afro-American Character and Destiny.* New York: Harper and Row.

Friedrich, Paul. 1970. *Agrarian Revolt in a Mexican Village.* Englewood Cliffs, New Jersey: Prentice-Hall.

——. 1986a. *The Princes of Naranja: An Essay in the Anthrohistorical Method.* Austin, Texas: University of Texas Press.

——. 1986b. *The Language Parallax: Linguistic Relativism and Poetic Indeterminacy.* Austin, Texas: University of Texas Press.

Gailey, Christine W. 1992. "Introduction: Civilization and Culture in the Work of Stanley Diamond," in Christine W. Gailey (ed.): *Dialectical Anthropology: Civilization in Crisis,* Vol.1. Essays in Honor of Stanley Diamond. Gainsville, Florida: University Press of Florida.

Gay, Peter. 1993. *The Cultivation of Hatred.* New York: W.W. Norton.

Geertz, Clifford. 1988. *Works and Lives: The Anthropologist as Author.* Stanford, California: Stanford University Press.

Gilroy, Paul. 1991 [1987]. *"There Ain't No Black in the Union Jack": The Cultural Politics of Race and Class.* Chicago: University of Chicago Press.

——. 1993a. *The Black Atlantic: Modernity and Double Consciousness.* Cambridge, Massachesetts: Harvard University Press.

——. 1993b. *Small Acts: Thoughts on the Politics of Black Cultures.* London: Serpent's Tail.

Gobineau, Joseph A. de. 1967 [1855]. *Essai sur l'inégalité des races humaines.* Paris: Pierre Belfond.

Godelier, Maurice. 1986 [1982]. *The Making of Great Men: Male Domination and Power among the New Guinea Baruya,* translated by Rupert Sawyer. Cambridge/Paris: Cambridge University Press/Éditions de la Maison des Sciences de l'homme.

Gould, Stephen J. 1981. *The Mismeasure of Man.* New York: W.W. Norton.

Gouldner, Alvin W. 1976. *The Dialectic of Ideology and Technology: The Origins, Grammar, and Future of Ideology.* London: Macmillan.

Gulliver, Pamela and Philip H. 1953. *The Central Nilo-Hamites.* London: International African Institute.

Hallpike, C.R. 1979. *The Foundations of Primitive Thought.* Oxford: The Clarendon Press.

Harden, Blaine. 1990. *Africa: Despatches From a Fragile Continent.* New York: W.W. Norton.

Harding, Sandra. 1989. "Taking Responsibility for Our Own Gender,

Race, Class: Transforming Science and the Social Studies of Science,"
Rethinking Marxism, 2:8–19.

Harding, Vincent. 1981. *There is a River: The Black Struggle for Freedom in America.* New York: Random House.

Harris, Marvin. 1968. *The Rise of Anthropological Theory: A History of Theories of Culture.* New York: Harper and Row.

Harrison, Faye V. 1988."Introduction: An African Diaspora Perspective for Urban Anthropology," *Urban Anthropology*, 17:111–41.

—— (ed.). 1991. *Decolonizing Anthropology: Moving Further Toward an Anthropology for Liberation.* Washington, D.C.: Association of Black Anthropologists/American Anthropological Association.

Hinde, Sidney and Hildegarde. 1901. *The Last of the Masai.* London: William Heinemann.

Huntingford, G.W.B. 1953. *The Southern Nilo-Hamites.* London: International African Institute.

Hymes, Dell. (ed.). 1969. *Reinventing Anthropology.* New York: Random House.

Jackson, Michael. 1989. *Paths Toward a Clearing: Radical Empiricism and Ethnographic Inquiry.* Bloomington, Indiana: Indiana University Press.

Jaffe, Hosea. 1985. *A History of Africa.* London: Zed Books Limited.

James, C.L.R. 1963 [1938]. *The Black Jacobins: Toussaint L'Ouverture and the San Domingo Revolution.* New York: Vintage Books.

Jarvie, Ian and Joseph Agassi. 1970. "The Problem of the Rationality of Magic," in Bryan Wilson (ed.). *Rationality.* New York: Harper and Row.

Jensen, Arthur R. 1969. "How Much Can We Boost IQ and Scholastic Achevement?" *Harvard Educational Review*, 33:1–13.

——. 1979. *Bias in Mental Testing.* New York: Free Press.

Jewsiewicki, Bogumil and David Newbury (eds). 1986. *African Historiographies: What History for Which Africa?* Beverly Hills, California: Sage Publications.

Katz, Walda and Irving Wainer. 1982. "A History of the Concept of Race; From Slavery to Reaganomics," *Science for The People*, 14:6–9, 31–3.

Kipuri, Naomi N. Ole. 1989. "Maasai Women in Transition: Class and Gender in the Transformation of a Pastoral Society." Philadelphia: Ph.D. Dissertation, Department of Anthropology, Temple University.

Knowles, Joan N. and David P. Collett. 1989. "Nature as Myth, Symbol and Action: Towards a Historical Understanding of Development and Conservation in Kenyan Maasailand," *Africa*, 59:433–60.

Kuklick, Henrietta. 1991. *The Savage Within: The Social History of British Anthropology, 1885–1945.* Cambridge: Cambridge University Press.

Kuper, Adam. 1973. *Anthropologists and Anthropology: The British School, 1925–1972.* London: Allen Lane.

——. 1988. *The Invention of the Primitive: Transformation of an Illusion.* London: Routledge.

Lee, Richard B. 1979. *The !Kung San: Men, Women, and Work in a Foraging Society.* Cambridge: Cambridge University Press.

Lefebvre, Henri. 1977. "Ideology and the Sociology of Knowledge," in Janet Dolgin, David Kemnitzer, and David M. Schneider (eds): *Symbolic Anthropology: A Reader in the Study of Symbols and Meanings.* New York: Columbia University Press.

Lenin, Vladimir I. 1970 [1917]. *Imperialism: The Highest Stage of Capitalism.* Moscow: Progress Publishers.

LePan, Don. 1989. *The Cognitive Revolution in Western Culture: The Birth of Expectation*, Vol.1. Basingstoke, Hampshire: Macmillan Press.

Lévi-Strauss, Claude. 1961. *Race et Histoire.* Paris: Editions Gonthier. Published in English as "Race and History," Chapter XVIII, in Claude Lévi-Strauss: *Structural Anthropology*, Vol.II, translated by Monique Layton. New York: Basic Books.

Lewontin, Richard C. 1982. "Are the Races Different?" *Science for the People*, 14:1–2, 10–14.

Lombroso, Cesare. 1887. *L'Homme criminel.* Paris: F. Alcan.

——. 1896. "Histoire des progrès de l'anthropologie et de la sociologie criminelles pendants les années 1895–1896," Geneva: *Trav. 4eme congrès internationale d'anthropologie criminelle*: 187–99.

Lukes, Steven. 1970. "Some Problems About Rationality," in Bryan Wilson (ed.): *Rationality.* New York: Harper and Row.

Lynn, Michael. 1989a. "Race Differences in Sexual Behavior: A Critique of Rushton and Bogaert's Evolutionary Hypothesis," *Journal of Research in Personality*, 32:1–6.

——. 1989b. "Criticisms of An Evolutionary Hypothesis About Race Differences: A Rebuttal to Rushton's Reply," *Journal of Research in Personality*, 23:21–34.

MacArthur, R.H. and E.O. Wilson. 1967. *The Theory of Island Biogeography.* Princeton, New Jersey: Princeton University Press.

Mafeje, Archie. 1970. "The Ideology of Tribalism," *Journal of Modern African Studies*, 9:253–61.

——. 1976. "The Problem of Anthropology in Historical Perspective: An Inquiry Into the Growth of the Social Sciences," *Canadian Journal of African Studies*, 10:307–33.

——. 1991. *The Theory and Ethnography of African Social Formations: The Case of the Interlacustrine Kingdoms.* London: CODESRIA Book Series.

Malinowski, Bronislaw. 1945. *The Dynamics of Culture Change: An Inquiry Into Race Relations in Africa.* New Haven: Connecticut: Yale University Press.

Manganaro, Marc (ed.). 1990. *Modernist Anthropology: From Fieldwork to Text.* Princeton, New Jersey: PrincetonUniversity Press.

Maquet, Jacques. 1961. *The Premise of Inequality in Rwanda: A Study of Political Relations in a Central African Kingdom.* London: Oxford University Press for the International African Institute.
——. 1971. *Power and Society in Africa.* London: Weidenfeld and Nicolson.
Marable, Manning. 1983. *How Capitalism Underdeveloped Black America: Problems in Race, Political Economy, and Society.* Boston, Massachusetts: South End Press.
——. 1992. *The Crisis in Color and Democracy: Essays on Race, Class and Power.* Monroe, Maine: Common Courage Press.
Marcus, George E. and Michael M. Fischer. 1986. *Anthropology as Cultural Critique: An Experimental Moment in the Human Sciences.* Chicago: University of Chicago Press.
Marcuse, Herbert. 1955 [1941]. *Reason and Revolution: Hegel and the Rise of Social Theory.* London: Routledge and Kegan Paul.
Marx, Karl. 1954 [1867]. *Capital*, Vol.1. Moscow: Progress Publishers.
Marx, Karl and Frederick Engels. 1970. *Selected Works*, Vol.3. Moscow: Progress Publishers.
McGrane, Bernard. 1989. *Beyond Anthropology: Society and the Other.* New York: Columbia University Press.
Miller, Christopher. 1985. *Blank Darkness: Africanist Discourse in French.* Chicago: University of Chicago Press.
——. 1990. *Theories of Africans: Francophone Literature and Anthropology in Africa.* Chicago: University of Chicago Press.
Mintz, Sidney W. 1974. *Caribbean Transformations.* New York: Columbia University Press.
Montagu, Ashley. 1964 [1942]. *Man's Most Dangerous Myth: The Fallacy of Race.* Cleveland, Ohio: World.
——. 1974. *The Concept of Race.* London: Collier Books.
——. 1975 (ed.). *Race and IQ.* New York: Oxford University Press.
Mudimbe, Valentin Y. 1991. *Parables and Fables: Exegesis, Textuality, and Politics in Central Africa.* Madison, Wisconsin: University of Wisconsin Press.
——. 1992 (ed.). *The Surreptitious Speech: "Présence Africaine" and the Politics of Otherness, 1947–1987.* Chicago: University of Chicago Press.
Mudimbe-Boyi, Elizabeth. 1992. "Harlem Renaissance and Africa: An Ambiguous Adventure," in V.Y. Mudimbe (ed.): *The Surreptitious Speech: "Présence Africaine" and the Politics of Otherness, 1947–1987.* Chicago: University of Chicago Press.
Nader, Laura. 1969. "Up the Anthropologist: Perspectives Gained From Studying Up," in Dell Hymes (ed.): *Reinventing Anthropology.* New York: Vintage Books.
Ngugi wa Thiong'o. 1981. *Writers in Politics.* London: Heinemann.
——. 1986. *Decolonising the Mind: The Politics of Language.* London/Nairobi: James Currey/Heinemann.

Oliver, Roland and Gervase Mathew (eds). 1963. *History of East Africa*, Vol.1. Oxford: The Clarendon Press.

Ouologuem, Yambo. 1971 [1968]. *Bound to Violence*, translated by Ralph Manheim. London: Heinemann.

Paine, Robert. 1971. "Animals as Capital," *Anthropological Quarterly*, 44:157–72.

Pandian, Jacob. 1985. *Anthropology and the Western Tradition: Toward an Authentic Anthropology*. Prospect Heights, Illinois: Waveland Press.

Patterson, Thomas and Frank Spencer. 1994. "Racial Hierarchies and Buffer Races," *Transforming Anthropology*, 5:20–7.

Patton, Cindy. 1992. "From Nation to Family: Containing 'African Aids'," in Andrew Parker, Mary Russo, Doris Sommer, and Patricia Yeager (eds): *Nationalisms and Sexualities*. New York: Routledge.

Posnansky, Merrick. 1966. "Kingship, Archaeology, and Historical Myth," *Uganda Journal*, 30:1–12.

Radliffe-Brown, Alfred R. 1952. *Structure and Function in Primitive Society*. London: Cohen and West.

Rigby, Peter. 1985. *Persistent Pastoralists: Nomadic Societies in Transition*. London: Zed Books Limited.

——. 1988a. "A Response to a Review of My Book, *Persistent Pastoralists: Nomadic Societies in Transition*," *American Anthropologist*, 90:418.

——. 1988b. "Class Formation Among East African Pastoralists: Maasai of Tanzania and Kenya," *Dialectical Anthropology*, 13:63–81.

——. 1989. "Ideology, Religion, and Ilparakuyo-Maasai Resistance to Capitalist Penetration," *Canadian Journal of African Studies*, 23:416–39.

——. 1991a. "Response to 'Anthropology and Marxist Discourse'," in V.Y. Mudimbe. *Parables and Fables: Exegesis, Textuality, and Politics in Central Africa*, pp.197–203. Madison, Wisconsin: The University of Wisconsin Press.

——. 1991b. "Anthropology, Revolution, and Development," a review article. *Reviews in Anthropology*, 19:231–9.

——. 1992a. *Cattle, Capitalism, and Class: Ilparakuyo-Maasai Transformations*. Philadelphia, Pennsylvania: Temple University Press.

——. 1992b. "Practical Ideology and Ideological Practice: On African Episteme and Marxian Problematic – Ilparakuyo Maasai Transformations," in V.Y. Mudimebe (ed.): *The Surreptitious Speech: "Présence Africaine" and the Politics of Otherness, 1947–1987*. Chicago: University of Chicago Press.

——. 1992c. "Africa, Epistemology, and Praxis: Aidan Southall's Unique Anthropology," in Hermine G. De Soto (ed.): *Culture and Contradiction: Dialectics of Wealth, Power, and Symbol*. San Francisco, California: EMTexts.

——. 1992d. "Review of *The World of Pastoralism: Herding Systems in Comparative Perspective*, by John. G. Galaty and Douglass L. Johnson (eds)." *American Anthropologist*, 94:730–1.

——. 1993. "Somalia, the U.S., and the Forgetting of History," *New Vision*, Kampala, 10 August 1993.

——. 1994. "Review of *Making a Market: The Institutional Transformation of an African Society*, by Jean Ensminger." *American Anthropologist*, 96:448–9.

Rodney, Walter. 1982 [1974]. *How Europe Underdeveloped Africa*. Washington, D.C.: Howard University Press.

Rose, Steven, Leon J. Kamin, and Richard C. Lewontin. 1984. *Not in Our Genes: Biology, Ideology, and Human Nature*. Harmondsworth: Penguin Books.

Rushton, J. Philippe. 1988. "Race Differences in Behavior: A Review and Evolutionary Hypothesis," *Personality and Individual Differences*, 9:1009–24.

——. 1985. "Differential K Theory: The Sociobiology of Individual and Group Differences," *Personality and Individual Differences*, 6:441–52.

——. 1989. "The Evolution of Racial Differences: A Response to M. Lynn," *Journal of Research in Personality*, 23:7–20.

Rushton, J. Philippe and A.F. Bogaert. 1987. "Race Differences in Sexual Behavior: Testing an Evolutionary Hypothesis," *Journal of Research in Personality*, 21:529–51.

Sacks, Karen B. 1993. "How Did Jews Become White?" (Unpublished M.S.)

Saitoti, Tepilit ole. 1980. *Maasai*. With photographs by Carol Beckwith. New York: Harry N. Abrams.

San Juan, E. Jr. 1992. *Racial Formations/Critical Transformations*. Atlantic Highlands, New Jersey: Humanities Press.

Sartre, Jean-Paul. 1948 [1947]. *Anti-Semite and Jew*, translated by Eric de Mauny. London: Secker and Warburg.

——. 1965 [1961]. "Preface", in Frantz Fanon: *The Wretched of The Earth*. London: MacGibbon and Key.

——. 1976 [1960]. *Critique of Dialectical Reason*, Vol.1, translated by Alan Sheridan-Smith. London: Verso.

Schmidt, Alfred. 1971. *The Concept of Nature in Marx*. London: New Left Books.

Schneider, Harold K. 1979. *Livestock and Equality in East Africa: The Economic Basis for Social Structure*. Bloomington, Indiana: Indiana University Press.

Seligman, C.G. and Brenda. 1932. *Pagan Tribes of the Nilotic Sudan*. London: Routledge and Kegan Paul. [Reissued 1965.]

Shanklin, Eugenia. 1994. *Anthropology and Race*. Belmont, California: Wadsworth.

Siwolop, Sana. 1991. "What's an Anthropologist Doing in My Office?", in Aaron Podolefsky and Peter J. Brown (eds): *Applying Cultural Anthropology*. Mountain View, California: Mayfield.

Snowden, Frank M. 1970. *Blacks in Antiquity: Ethiopians in the Greco-Roman Experience.* Cambridge, Massachusetts: Belknap Press.

——. 1983. *Before Color Prejudice: The Ancient View of Blacks.* Cambridge, Massachusetts: Harvard University Press.

Southall, Aidan W. 1960. "Homicide and Suicide Among the Alur," in Paul Bohannan (ed.): *African Homicide and Suicide.* Princeton, New Jersey: Princeton University Press.

——. 1966. "The Peopling of Africa: The Linguistic and Sociological Evidence," in Merrick Posnansky (ed.): *Prelude to East African History.* London/Nairobi: Oxford University Press.

——. 1970. "The Illusion of Tribe," in Peter Gutkind (ed.): *The Passing of Tribal Man in Africa.* Leiden: E.J. Brill.

——. 1985. "The Ethnic Heart of Anthropology," a review article. *Cahiers d'Etudes africaines,* 20:567–72.

Sowell, Thomas. 1983. *The Economics and Politics of Race.* New York: William Morrow.

——. 1984. *Civil Rights: Rhetoric or Reality?* New York: Basic Books.

Spencer, Paul. 1984. "Pastoralism and the Ghost of Capitalism," *Production pastorale et société,* 15:61–76.

——. 1988. *The Maasai of Matapato: A Study of Rituals of Rebellion.* Bloomington, Indiana: Indiana University Press for the International African Institute.

Stepan, Nancy. 1982. *The Idea of Race in Science: Great Britain, 1800–1960.* Hamden, Connecticut: Archon Books.

Stinson-Fernandez, John. 1994. "Conceptualizing Culture and Ethnicity: Toward an Anthropology of Puerto Rican Philadelphia." Philadelphia: Ph.D. Dissertation, Department of Anthropology, Temple University.

St. John, Spencer. 1884. *Hayti: Or the Black Republic.* London: Smith and Elder.

Stocking, George W. 1968. *Race, Culture, and Evolution: Essays in the History of Anthropology.* New York: The Free Press. [Republished with a new Preface, 1982.]

Stoller, Paul. 1989. *The Taste of Ethnographic Things: The Senses in Anthropology.* Philadelphia, Pennsylvania: University of Pennsylvania Press.

Taylor, Ian, P. Walton and J. Young. 1978. *The New Criminology: For a Social Theory of Deviance.* London: Routledge and Kegan Paul.

Temu, Arnold and Bonaventure Swai. 1981. *Historians and Africanist History: A Critique.* London: Zed Press.

Traweek, Susan. 1988. *Beamtimes and Lifetimes: The World of High Energy Physicists.* Cambridge, Massachusetts: Harvard University Press.

Trouillot, Michel-Rolph. 1990. *Haiti, State Against Nation: The Origins and Legacy of Duvalierism.* New York: Monthly Review.

van Binsbergen, Wim and Peter Geschiere (eds). 1985. *Old Modes of*

Production and Capitalist Encroachment: Anthropological Explorations in Africa. London: KPI Limited

Waller, Richard. 1976. "The Maasai and the British, 1895–1905: The Origins of an Alliance," *Journal of African History*, 17:529–53.

Walvin, James. 1973. *Black and White: The Negro and English Society, 1555–1945*. London: Allen Lane.

Whitney, Glayde. 1990. "On Possible Genetic Bases of Race Differences in Criminality," in Lee Ellis and Harry Hoffman (eds): *Crime in Biological, Social, and Moral Contexts*. New York: Praeger.

Will, George. 1991. "Nature and the Male Sex," *Newsweek*, 17 June, p.70.

Williams, Raymond. 1958. *Culture and Society: 1780–1950*. New York: Columbia University Press.

——. 1977. *Marxism and Literature*. Oxford: Oxford University Press.

Willis, William S. 1969. "Skeletons in the Anthropological Closet," in Dell Hymes (ed.): *Reinventing Anthropology*. New York: Vintage Books.

Wilson, Bryan (ed.). 1970. *Rationality*. New York: Harper and Row.

Wilson, James Q. 1991. *On Character*. Washington, D.C.: AEI Press.

Wilson, James Q. and P.J. Cross. 1985. "Unemployment and Crime: What is the Connection?" *Public Interest*, 79:3–8.

Wilson, James Q. and Richard J. Herrnstein. 1985. *Crime and Human Nature*. New York: Simon and Schuster.

Zuckerman, M. 1990. "Some Dubious Premises in Research and Theory on Racial Differences," *American Psychologist*, 45:1297–1303.

Zuckerman, M. and N. Brody. 1988. "Oysters, Rabbits, and People: A Critique of 'Race Differences in Behavior' by J.P. Rushton," *Personality and Individual Differences*. 9:1025–33.

Index

Perry Anderson "In the Tracks of
                 Historical Materialism" 1984

Kwame A. Appiah - "In My Father's House"
                    1994

Talal Asad "Genealogies of Religion"
            - DIVINATION? 1993

William Cohen - "French Encounter
                 1980   "/ African"

J. Conrad - Heart of Darkness

F. Fanon - The Wretched of the Earth

J. Ensminger - "Making a Market"
                 1992.

Le MERIDIEN

Starboard
H: 13-21½   W: 16¼-20¼ W

Port (2)
H: 16¼-17   W: 18½-22 W

Port (1)
H ~~16¼-17~~ 33½-35   W 18½-22 W

Port (1) Sun Mark/Fading
19×24
H   W

ł